An Information and Construction of Law

---

*An Information and Construction of Law
to recommend the general liberty
advanced by the Declaration of Independence
and reserved to the people by the Constitution
for the United States of America*

ISBN 978-1-304-40360-5

CONTENTS

Introduction

The United States were once revered; now it is not. The structure of the previous sentence suggests the very problem; what once was a compound republic becomes a singular state, a democratic society, what the founders called a *national society*.

Much has been made of the democratical nature of the United States, but one of the bright ideas of the framers of the Constitution was to divorce government from the passions of the people. This dissociation of elections and rights may be their greatest achievement. They created a political system where fundamental rights are never votable, but are instead permanently secured by higher law, kept out of reach of the electoral process and beyond mere legislation. This is our success, inherited from *We the People of the United States*, who put their confidence in God.

Today our federalism is up against a political class with a mobbish self-confidence that comes across like an offer that cannot be refused.

Accepting those rules and regulations offered by the national state produces consequences, however, the most insidious of which is that the relationship between citizen and government becomes equitable rather than legal, and that relationship is then adjudged according to equitable principles rather than law as such.[i] This disadvantages the citizen forensically, as it considers those protections guaranteed by law and recasts them in a compromising light, or displaces them altogether.

---

[i] *Wickard v. Filburn*, 317 U.S. 111, 129-133 (1942).

It was once written that "the facility and excess of law-making seem to be the diseases to which our governments are most liable,"[ii] which would help to explain today's drive toward a comprehensive regulatory construct governing every element of human behavior. Our government is now an enormous engine for battering down the Constitution as if en route to a perfect national electorate of the sort that may even vote the government apart -- coalitional government of the type that may "fall" or be "brought down" by an election result -- government not of laws, but of men.

As this United States degenerates from mere nuisance to outright nemesis, it makes sense to think about your own freedom, where it came from, how it can be kept.

The Declaration of Independence created thirteen several States, constitutionally indistinct and peopled by equal sovereigns, just as equality under the law remains the hallmark of our system. The people of these states created a brand new sovereign called the *United States*, the nature and extent of which were defined in the Constitution, which even the people can amend only when convened in their individual states. In this way we protect ourselves against our own passing fancies and preserve basic freedoms by excluding a national society from any part in our government. Despite all the noise, Americans have never amended this core constitutional principle of legal equality. Law is the same for everyone.

So it remains that a law waived for some of us is no law at all, just as a law that prefers members of the government is no law at all.

[ii] *The Federalist* No. 62, at 378 (James Madison) (Clinton Rossiter ed., 1961).

And a nation of the government, by the government, for the government, is no nation at all.

I write to thank you for supporting the Declaration of Independence and the Constitution of the United States, safeguards for our "new nation, conceived in liberty, and dedicated to the proposition that all men are created equal."*iii*

Please accept this citizen survey of the United States to appreciate your support, and to celebrate the birth of our United States on July 4, 1776.

---

iii Abraham Lincoln, *The Gettysburg Address* para. 1 (November 19, 1863).

"Four score and seven years ago our fathers brought forth on this continent a new nation, conceived in liberty, and dedicated to the proposition that all men are created equal.

Now we are engaged in a great civil war, testing whether that nation, or any nation so conceived and so dedicated, can long endure. We are met on a great battlefield of that war. We have come to dedicate a portion of that field, as a final resting place for those who here gave their lives that that nation might live. It is altogether fitting and proper that we should do this.

But, in a larger sense, we can not dedicate, we can not consecrate, we can not hallow this ground. The brave men, living and dead, who struggled here, have consecrated it, far above our poor power to add or detract. The world will little note, nor long remember what we say here, but it can never forget what they did here. It is for us the living, rather, to be dedicated here to the unfinished work which they who fought here have thus far so nobly advanced. It is rather for us to be here dedicated to the great task remaining before us — that from these honored dead we take increased devotion to that cause for which they gave the last full measure of devotion — that we here highly resolve that these dead shall not have died in vain — that this nation, under God, shall have a new birth of freedom — and that government of the people, by the people, for the people, shall not perish from the earth." *Id.* in toto.

INFORMATION AND CONSTRUCTION OF LAW

It has cost me many a Sleepless Night to find out the most obnoxious Part of the proposed Plan.—And I have finally fixed upon the exclusive Legislation in the Ten Miles Square.

And have not this supreme Legislature a Right to naturalize me there; whether I will or not?

May not the sovereign of the Country, Grant exclusive Privilidges to all that are willing to be naturalized in that hallowed Spot?

American patriot Samuel Osgood wrote these words in a letter to fellow revolutionary Samuel Adams in January, 1788,[1] reflecting a suspicion toward *any* national territory perhaps lost on contemporary observers. As one noted legal authority asked in 1899, "What extent of territory do the United States of America comprise? In order to answer this question intelligently, it is necessary to ascertain the meaning of the term 'United States.'"[2] The answer has never meant more.

---

[1] Bernard Bailyn, *The Debate on the Constitution, Part One* 704 (1993).
[2] C.C. Langdell, *The Status of Our New Territories*, 12 Harv. L. Rev. 365, 365 (1899).

Today, the grave issue is whether our United States will become a consolidated government absolute in its jurisdiction, with the people exercising their rights and powers by its sufferance, or remain a union of states and a nation of people as intended by the framers.[3]

---

[3] James Madison's report of the "Debates in the Federal Convention of 1787." The compromise between the sovereignty of the states and the sovereignty of the people over all results in a "union of states" and a "nation of people." "This is the distilled essence of our republican form of government." *Harris v. Anderson*, 194 Kan. 302, 318 (Fatzer, J., dissenting) (1965). Madison's writings, especially his convention notes, are advised. Thomas Jefferson acknowledged to John Adams in 1815, "Do you know that there exists in manuscript the ablest work of this kind ever yet executed, of the debates of the constitutional convention of Philadelphia in 1788? The whole of every thing said and done there was taken down by Mr. Madison, with a labor and exactness beyond comprehension." 3 Max Farrand, *The Records of the Federal Convention of 1787* 421 (1911). "The affairs of the United States, he perhaps, has the most correct knowledge of, of any Man in the Union." (William Pierce: Character Sketches of Delegates to the Federal Convention). 3 *id*. at 94.

Abstract of American Law

God attends American jurisprudence as the source of our unalienable rights and is recognized as our Creator[4] by the "unanimous Declaration of the thirteen united States of America" in Congress, July 4, 1776.[5]

Armed revolution sustained their declaration, and the successful termination of the War of Independence proved them to be thirteen "Free and Independent States," each replete with the attributes of sovereignty, each with a people, a territory and government of its own, all together a "teeming nation of nations"[6] chartered under common law.

In addition, "when a new State is admitted into the Union, it is so admitted with all of the powers of sovereignty and jurisdiction which pertain to the original States...."[7] Thus, in legal contemplation, each one of America's fifty States is primarily "free, sovereign and independent" as conceded.[8] In this way "'Both the States and the United States existed before the Constitution[,]'"[9] when no part of the American governmental system was held in common by all of the people of the United States.

---

[4] *God* is defined as "the creator, and the sovereign of the Universe." 1 Noah Webster, *An American Dictionary of the English Language* 93 (1828).

[5] "We hold these truths to be self-evident, that all men are created equal, that they are endowed by their Creator with certain unalienable Rights, that among these are Life, Liberty and the pursuit of Happiness." *The Declaration of Independence* para. 2 (U.S. 1776).

[6] Walt Whitman, *Leaves of Grass* iii (1855).

[7] *Coyle v. Oklahoma*, 221 U.S. 559, 573 (1911).

[8] Definitive Treaty of Peace, September 3, 1783, U.S.-Gr. Brit., T.S. No. 104, Article 1. Notice how Britain conceded all territorial rights to the United States -- namely, to each State.

[9] *New York v. United States*, 505 U.S. 144, 162 (1992) (quoting *Lane County v. Oregon*, 7 Wall. 71, 76 (1869)).

Conventional compromise amid perfect States or a perfect Nation resulted in a partial eclipse of State sovereignty, and a more perfect United States under the Constitution than under the existing Articles of Confederation:[10]

> In a word; the two extremes before us are a perfect separation & a perfect incorporation, of the 13 States. In the first case they would be independent nations subject to no law, but the law of nations. In the last, they would be mere counties of one entire republic, subject to one common law.[11]

The people engrafted federal jurisdiction on to their extant common-law States "in Order to form a more perfect Union," rather than to consolidate the Union into one government absolute in its jurisdiction.[12] After all, "the local or municipal authorities form distinct and independent portions of the supremacy...."[13]

"Our federalism" delimitates a *compound* republic, a system designed to divide government power and reserve the broad liberty jurisdiction to the people.[14] "For when the Revolution took place, the people of each state became themselves sovereign...."[15]

---

[10] "We have seen that in the new government, as in the old, the general powers are limited...." *The Federalist* No. 40, at 251 (James Madison) (Clinton Rossiter ed., 1961).

[11] 1 Max Farrand, *The Records of the Federal Convention of 1787* 449 (James Madison) (1911).

[12] United States Const. pmbl.

[13] *The Federalist* No. 39, at 245 (James Madison) (Clinton Rossiter ed., 1961).

[14] *The Federalist* No. 51, at 323 (James Madison) (Clinton Rossiter ed., 1961).

[15] *Martin v. Waddell*, 41 U.S. 367, 410 (1842).

As an incidence of the sovereignty created when this country achieved its independence, "the prerogatives of the crown devolved upon the people of the States. And this power still remains with them, except so far as they have delegated a portion of it to the federal government."[16]

Any true survey of law comprehends its affinity for territory,[17] suggested by the very term "law of the land," and correlates the limited extent of United States territory, which the Constitution always identifies as the territory of the States.[18] Along those lines, our nation's high court has long held the source of an American's fundamental rights to be State law, not United States law.[19]

No wonder that "Federal privileges and immunities may seem limited in their formulation by comparison with the expansive definition given to the privileges and immunities attributed to state citizenship...."[20] There is no territory under the Union.

In American law, the people of the Union delegated the powers of national sovereignty by particulars, limited to certain subject matters, rather than by broad territorial cession. Remarkably, admitting a State into the Union has the effect to *withdraw* from federal jurisdiction all the territory within the boundaries of the new State.[21]

---

[16] *Fontain v. Ravenel*, 58 U.S. 369, 384 (1854).

[17] "The boundary line is the line of sovereignty," *Central R.R. Co. v. Jersey City*, 209 U.S. 473, 478 (1908). "We repeat that boundary means sovereignty," *id.* at 479.

[18] C.C. Langdell, *The Status of Our New Territories*, 12 Harv. L. Rev. 365, 368 (1899).

[19] *Slaughterhouse Cases*, 83 U.S. 36 (1873).

[20] *U.S. Term Limits, Inc. v. Thornton*, 514 U.S. 779, 844 (1995) (Kennedy, J., concurring).

[21] *Fort Leavenworth R.R. Co. v. Lowe*, 114 U.S. 525, 527-531 (1885).

The sovereignty of a body politic commonly extends to *all* of the valid subjects of lawful government within its territorial jurisdiction.[22] This is even true of the United States pursuant to Article 1, § 8, clause 17, where we find out the only geographic area ceded from the States to the United States is at the seat of government.

This makes Washington, D.C., the extent of durable national territory, realizing the complete power of the Nation, to be exercised over *all* the legitimate subjects of lawful government, but reaching only the District of Columbia and like places.[23] As to United States authority among the several States, "The powers delegated by the proposed Constitution to the federal government are few and defined."[24]

By design, then, a comprehensive national power is prohibited generally, although the District of Columbia is "constitutionally distinct from the States."[25]

Evidently, certain underlying features inherent in the Constitution support the common sense of that instrument to confirm that the United States are so a union of states and a nation of people as reported.[26]

---

[22] Thomas M. Cooley, *Constitutional Limitations* 4 (6th Ed. 1890).

[23] The District of Columbia et al. "are the only cases, within the United States, in which all the powers of government are united in a single government," *Pollard's Lessee v. Hagan*, 44 U.S. 212, 223 (1845).

[24] "Those which are to remain in the State governments are numerous and indefinite." *The Federalist* No. 45, at 292 (James Madison) (Clinton Rossiter ed., 1961).

[25] *Palmore v. United States*, 411 U.S. 389, 395, 397-398 (1973).

[26] *See generally* Max Farrand, *The Records of the Federal Convention of 1787* (1911).

"Union of States"

These *United States* began, famously, on July 4, 1776. Collectively, they are limited to certain delegated powers enumerated in the Constitution.[27] The enumeration incorporated no State territory, except for areas like the "ten Miles square" surveyed *infra*. This means the people retained the common-law republics embraced by State lines, and never delegated any common law to the United States in general (except the Constitution itself).[28]

> [T]he preservation of the States, and the maintenance of their governments, are as much within the design and care of the Constitution as the preservation of the Union and the maintenance of the National government. The Constitution, in all its provisions, looks to an indestructible Union, composed of indestructible States.[29]

> No political dreamer was ever wild enough to think of breaking down the lines which separate the states, and of compounding the American people into one common mass.[30]

---

[27] U.S. Const. art. 1, § 8. U.S. Const. amends. IX, X.

[28] "There is no federal general common law." *Erie R.R. Co. v. Tompkins*, 304 U.S. 64, 78 (1938). "The common law is not a brooding omnipresence in the sky" but "always is the law of some State," not the States *en bloc*. *Southern Pacific v. Jenson*, 244 U.S. 205, 222 (Holmes, J., dissenting) (1917).

[29] *Texas v. White*, 74 U.S. 700, 725 (1868). It remains legally impossible to destroy the United States or any of them. On the other hand, national governments typically fall by ballot, whereby elections may bring down the government rather than merely change or maintain its administration.

[30] "Of consequence, when they act, they act in their States." *McCulloch v. State*, 17 U.S. 316, 403 (1819).

At the time the American people established the Constitution, they withheld their State territory from the new sovereign to retain for themselves "those fundamental rights of person and property attached to citizenship by the common law and enactments of the states."[31]

As the *Federalist*[32] emphasizes, although *operation* of United States law is "national, not federal," *jurisdiction* of United States law is "federal, not national,"[33] the term *federal* referring to the American Union of the *States*, the term *national* more strictly synonymous with *people.*[34]

The very structure of the Constitution precludes extensive authority over the people of the States by withholding the sort of national jurisdiction claimed by every other national society in world history.

In law, jurisdiction is always considered first.[35]

---

[31] *Hague v. C.I.O.*, 307 U.S. 496, 521 n.1 (1939). Defining these rights fully calls for external referents, such as *Commentaries on the Laws of England* by William Blackstone, "whose works constituted the preeminent authority on English law for the founding generation." *Alden v. Maine*, 527 U.S. 706, 715 (1999).

[32] A series of essays titled *The Federalist Papers* was published while the Constitution was before the country for adoption or rejection. Two of its authors helped to frame the Constitution. "The opinion of the *Federalist* has always been considered as of great authority. It is a complete commentary on our constitution; and is appealed to by all parties in the questions to which that instrument has given birth. Its intrinsic merit entitles it to this high rank," *Cohens v. Virginia*, 19 U.S. 264, 418 (1821).

[33] *The Federalist* No. 39, at 246 (James Madison) (Clinton Rossiter ed., 1961).

[34] Thomas M. Cooley, *Constitutional Limitations* 3 (6th Ed. 1890).

[35] "*Jurisdiction*, in its most general sense, is the power to make, declare or apply the law," and "is limited to place or territory, to persons, or to particular subjects." 2 Noah Webster, *An American Dictionary of the English Language* 2 (1828).

"Nation of People"

The people set forth this *United States* to become the name of the new sovereign created by the Constitution.[36]

They excised an area "not exceeding ten Miles square" to be "the Seat of the Government of the United States," granting Congress power over it, "To exercise exclusive Legislation in all Cases whatsoever."[37] Here, "Exclusive legislative power is in essence complete sovereignty."[38] Despite "complete authority at the seat of government"[39] the Constitution still withholds from Congress "a general police power of the sort retained by the States."[40]

> This grant of comprehensive legislative power over certain areas of the Nation, when read in conjunction with the rest of the Constitution, further confirms that Congress was not ceded plenary authority over the *whole* Nation.[41]

The Supreme Court has always declined to convert congressional authority under the Commerce Clause into "a plenary police power that would authorize enactment of every type of legislation."[42]

---

[36] Our national state came to be on June 21, 1788, when the Constitution went into effect.

[37] U.S. Const. art. I, § 8, cl. 17.

[38] *S.R.A., Inc. v. State of Minnesota*, 327 U.S. 558, 562 (1946).

[39] *The Federalist* No. 43, at 272 (James Madison) (Clinton Rossiter ed., 1961).

[40] *United States v. Lopez*, 514 U.S. 549, 567 (1995).

[41] *United States v. Lopez*, 514 U.S. 549, 589 n.3 (1995) (Thomas, J., concurring).

[42] *United States v. Lopez*, 514 U.S. 549, 566 (1995).

Authoritative historical opinion is clear that when contemplated in relation to the extent of its powers "the proposed Government cannot be deemed a *national* one; since its jurisdiction extends to certain enumerated objects only, and leaves to the several States a residuary and inviolable sovereignty over all other objects."[43]

The Constitution prohibits Congress from exercising exclusive legislation throughout the country, because "States are not mere political subdivisions of the United States."[44] Nor are their citizens simply political constituents of the national forum. Americans today are descendants of the people of the original Union, the "posterity" of their Constitution. As successors to the blessings of liberty referred to in the preamble, the common law is our birthright and our inheritance.

Moreover, the critical postulate that sovereignty is *reserved to the people* distinguishes those citizens from mere national subjects:

> It will be admitted on all hands, that with the exception of the powers surrendered by the Constitution of the United States, the people of the several States are absolutely and unconditionally sovereign within their respective territories.[45]

---

[43] *The Federalist* No. 39, at 245 (James Madison) (Clinton Rossiter ed., 1961). "Were it wholly national, the supreme and ultimate authority would reside in the *majority* of the people of the Union; and this authority would be competent at all times, like that of a majority of every national society to alter or abolish its established Government." *Id.* at 246.

[44] *New York v. United States*, 505 U.S. 144, 188 (1992).

[45] *Ohio Life Ins. and Trust Co. v. Debolt*, 57 U.S. 416, 428 (1853).

So consider the articulation of States which form and occupy our Union. See the people there.

Then consider that "sovereignty is mainly territorial, unless a different meaning clearly appears."[46] Notice as well that this "sovereignty of the States" is designed exclusively "for the protection of individuals," not for the benefit of the States or state governments, or even the public officials governing the States.[47]

At the heart of the matter, "The constitution of the United States was ordained and established, not by the states in their sovereign capacities, but emphatically, as the preamble of the constitution declares, by 'the people of the United States.'" It follows that the people had a right "to reserve to themselves those sovereign authorities which they might not choose to delegate to either" government.[48]

By the Declaration of Independence, aforesaid God grants these rights; governments are instituted to secure them. This revolutionary end was accomplished when the country ratified the Constitution, establishing its novel system of coordinate sovereigns.

Divided authority is based on the assumption that in division there is not only strength but freedom from tyranny.[49] Often missed in the American dialectic between Union and Nation is this point, that "State sovereignty is not just an end in itself: 'Rather, federalism secures to citizens the liberties that derive from the diffusion of sovereign power.'"[50]

---

[46] *Central R.R. Co. v. Jersey City*, 209 U.S. 473, 479 (1908).

[47] *New York v. United States*, 505 U.S. 144, 181 (1992).

[48] *Martin v. Hunter's Lessee*, 14 U.S. 304, 324-325 (1816).

[49] *Reid v. Covert*, 354 U.S. 1, 40 (1957).

[50] *New York v. United States*, 505 U.S. 144, 181 (1992) (quoting *Coleman v. Thompson*, 501 U.S. 722, 759 (1991) (Blackmun, J., dissenting)).

On the other hand, nationalism detracts from citizens the liberties informed by their common law, ramparted by their States, and guaranteed by their United States. Against the resulting confusion of sovereign power, the American people comprise a land of the lost.

If instead the United States are "the land of the free" as anthemed, then each one of them safeguards its geographic portion of the supremacy.

In the United States,[51] liberty goes with the territory.

---

[51] "The term 'United States' may be used in any one of several senses." It may be "the collective name of the states which are united by and under the Constitution." Since the adoption of the Constitution, it has also been "merely the name of a sovereign occupying the position analogous to that of other sovereigns in the family of nations. It may designate the territory over which the sovereignty of the United States extends," *Hooven & Allison Co. v. Evatt*, 324 U.S. 652, 671-672 (1945). Therefore, "the conclusion is that the meaning which that term had the day after Independence was declared, it still retains, and that this is its natural and literal meaning." C.C. Langdell, *The Status of Our New Territories*, 12 Harv. L. Rev. 365, 368 (1899). "It will be seen, therefore, that, while the United States, in its second sense, signifies the body politic created by the Constitution, in its first sense it signifies the members of that body politic in the aggregate. A consequence is that, while in its first sense the term 'United States' is always plural, in its second sense it is in strictness always singular." *Id.* at 369. "It is very important, however, to understand that the use of the term 'United States' to designate all territory over which the United States is sovereign, is, like the similar use of the word 'empire' in England and other European countries, purely conventional; and that it has, therefore, no legal or constitutional significance. Indeed, this use of the term has no connection whatever with the Constitution of the United States....

The conclusion, therefore, is that, while the term 'United States' has three meanings, only the first and second of these are known to the Constitution; and that is equivalent to saying that the Constitution of the United States as such does not extend beyond the limits of the States which are united by and under it," *id.* at 371.

AN INFORMATION AND CONSTRUCTION OF LAW

The Common Law

Among the most elementary of our legal concepts is that of the adoption of the English common law as the basis of American jurisprudence. The *common law* is all the statutory and case law background of England and the American Colonies before the American Revolution.[52] This "birthright" of inherited rights came down through history from 1215 and the Great Charter, its binding force independent of written or statute law.

> That body of rules, principles and customs which have been received from our ancestors, and by which courts have been governed in their judicial decisions. The evidence of this law is to be found in the reports of those decisions, and the records of the courts.[53]

> Those who emigrated to this country from England brought with them this great privilege "as their birthright and inheritance, as a part of that admirable common law which had fenced around and interposed barriers on every side against the approaches of arbitrary power."[54]

Fortunately for us, each of the new states promptly adopted the existing body of English common law.

---

[52] *Black's Law Dictionary* 276 (6th ed. 1990).

[53] 1 Noah Webster, *An American Dictionary of the English Language* 42 (1828).

[54] *Thompson v. Utah*, 170 U.S. 343, 349-350 (1898) (quoting 2 Story, Const. § 1779). "Our ancestors were entitled to the common law of England when they emigrated," as they pleased. C. Bradley Thompson, *The Revolutionary Writings of John Adams* 238 (2000).

The common law proved to be "the best foundation on which to erect an enduring structure of civil liberty which the world has ever known. It was the peculiar excellence of the common law of England that it recognized the worth, and sought especially to protect the rights and privileges, of the individual man."[55]

> It fills up every interstice, and occupies every wide space which the statute law cannot occupy..."we live in the midst of the common law, we inhale it at every breath, imbibe it at every pore; we meet with it when we wake and when we lay down to sleep, when we travel and when we stay at home; and it is interwoven with the very idiom that we speak; and we cannot learn another system of laws without learning, at the same time, another language."[56]

Under no system of law is personal liberty more potent and a free State more secure than under that system known as the common law. The whole structure of our present jurisprudence stands upon the original foundation of the common law.

---

[55] Thomas M. Cooley, *Constitutional Limitations* 33 (6th Ed. 1890). Furthermore, "arbitrary power and uncontrolled authority were not recognized in its principles. Awe surrounded and majesty clothed the king, but the humblest subject might shut the door of his cottage against him, and defend from intrusion that privacy which was as sacred as the kingly prerogatives. The system was the opposite of servile; its features implied boldness and independent self-reliance on the part of the people...." *Id.*
[56] James Kent, *Commentaries on American Law* Lecture 16 (1826) (quoting Du Ponceau on Jurisdiction, p. 91).

The best evidence of this "unwritten law" may be extracted from our charter documents, judicial opinions and the sources upon which the courts themselves rely. "Of course, 'Blackstone's Commentaries are accepted as the most satisfactory exposition of the common law of England.... [U]ndoubtedly the framers of the Constitution were familiar with it.'"[57]

This matters because the legal interpretation of the Constitutional text can only be made by consulting the common law, the principles, history and terminology of which were close to the people, and the first Congress. "The language of the Constitution, as has been well said, could not be understood without reference to the common law."[58]

> There is no common law of the United States, in the sense of a national customary law, distinct from the common law of England as adopted by the several States each for itself, applied as its local law, and subject to such alteration as may be provided by its own statutes....
>
> There is, however, one clear exception to the statement that there is no national common law. The interpretation of the Constitution of the United States is necessarily influenced by the fact that its provisions are framed in the language of the English common law, and are to be read in the light of its history.[59]

---

[57] *Bloom v. State of Illinois*, 391 U.S. 194, 199 n.2 (1968) (quoting *Schick v. United States*, 195 U.S. 65, 69 (1904)).

[58] *United States v. Wong Kim Ark*, 169 U.S. 649, 654 (1898).

[59] *Smith v. Alabama*, 124 U.S. 465, 478 (1888).

The common-law prerogatives reassured by the Ninth and Tenth Amendments of the Constitution include those rights "retained by the people" and those powers "reserved to the States respectively, or to the people" under this instrument, "the adoption of which, was in its day, regarded a prodigy."[60] Both articles confirm rights and powers that reckon July 4, 1776, to ratification of the Constitution, guarding its successors against legislative innovation.[61] American freedom is our success, because "the common law is the best and most common birthright that the subject hath, for the safeguard and defence of his rights of person and property."[62] Common-law rights are as familiar as the Bill of Rights itself, as basic as life, liberty and property; the right to speak freely and travel about, or to be left alone; to earn a living, to contract and to socialize; to due process and the jury. They comprise the general liberty, and must include "the natural right of resistance and self-preservation...."[63]

---

[60] James DeWitt Andrews, *American Law and Procedure* Vol. XIII, *Jurisprudence and Legal Institutions* 243 (1913). Enumerated objects of control and authoritative judicial review "present the unique and striking features of the American constitution," *id.*

[61] "Fear of federal encroachment led to the adoption of the Ninth and Tenth Amendments, which, if they did not weaken the instrument, were intended to prevent its expansion by legislation. By the Ninth Amendment it is declared that the enumeration of certain rights shall not be construed to deny others retained by the people, while the Tenth Amendment reserves to the people or the states those powers not expressly granted to the government and not expressly forbidden to the states. These two amendments not only satisfied the opponents of nationalism but did much to give the Constitution a rigidity which has kept the system close to the letter of the original document." Everett Kimball, *The National Government of the United States* 40 (1920).

[62] *Strother v. Lucas*, 37 U.S. 410, 437 (1838).

[63] 1 William Blackstone, *Commentaries* *139. "This natural life being... the immediate donation of the great creator," 1 *id.* at *129.

As there are two distinct systems of law in the world, the advancement of any people will be determined in large part by whether the underlying principles of the English *Common Law* or those of the Roman *Civil Law* are adopted.[64]

Though the legal systems of the individual States are primarily based upon the common law, there is no national equivalent other than the Constitution itself. The United States government is a *civil law* state, a singular national community elaborating, like other of the world's civilian nations, upon Roman law; but apart from the operation of their national government, allegiance to the common law has been characteristic of the American people. Constitutional authority that the common law belongs to the people of the United States is plain,[65] even conspicuous in the Seventh Amendment.

The most important characteristic of the common law is the recognition, not merely theoretical, but practical, of equality before the law, though not actually taken up in the sovereignty of any people on earth until it was announced in our Declaration of Independence, and put on general exhibit.[66]

---

[64] Emlin McClain, *The Civil and the Common Law in the Louisiana Purchase* 7 (1905).

[65] "What could the Convention have done? If they had in general terms declared the Common law to be in force, they would have broken in upon the legal Code of every State in the most material points...." 3 Max Farrand, *The Records of the Federal Convention of 1787* 130 (James Madison) (1911).

[66] "The spirit which everywhere displayed itself at the commencement of the struggle, and which vanquished the obstacles to independence, is the best of proofs that a sufficient portion of liberty had been everywhere enjoyed to inspire both a sense of its worth and a zeal for its proper enlargement." *The Federalist* No. 52, at 329 (James Madison) (Clinton Rossiter ed., 1961).

By "sovereignty" in its constitutional sense is meant the supreme law, the absolute rule of action and decision for the government and all its parts. In the United States, the primary source of sovereignty became their people.[67] They delegated only certain powers to the public domain, still controlling its career by way of the republican form of government guaranteed in the Constitution.[68]

Noah Webster was a contemporary of the founding fathers and a commissioned publicist of the federalist cause. His lexicon of 1828 remains a fundamental text and a unique repository of the original meaning of terms used in the founding years of this nation:

SOVEREIGN, *a.*
1. Supreme in power; possessing supreme dominion; as a *sovereign* prince. God is the *sovereign* ruler of the universe.
2. Supreme; superior to all others; chief. God is the *sovereign* good of all who love and obey him.

SOVEREIGNTY, *n.*
Supreme power; supremacy; the possession of the highest power, or of uncontrollable power. Absolute *sovereignty* belongs to God only.[69]

---

[67] "The very meaning of sovereignty is that the decree of the sovereign makes law." *American Banana Co. v. United Fruit Co.*, 213 U.S. 347, 358 (1909).

[68] U.S. Const. art. IV, § 4. "The genius of republican liberty seems to demand on one side not only that all power should be derived from the people, but that those intrusted with it should be kept in dependence on the people...." *The Federalist* No. 37, at 227 (James Madison) (Clinton Rossiter ed., 1961).

[69] 2 Noah Webster, *An American Dictionary of the English Language* 76 (1828).

Having secured this God-given sovereignty against the Crown of England in 1776, the people entrusted part of it to their respective States and, more recently, to the new United States of the Constitution.[70]

They kept the rest by devising their constitution to effectively protect the many rights which antecede that document and even the States themselves,[71] and avoided the dangers of a national police power by restricting its operation to the seat of the government, and those "territories and possessions" belonging to the United States.[72]

> Generally speaking, within any State of this Union the preservation of the peace and the protection of person and property are the functions of the state government, and are no part of the primary duty, at least, of the nation. The laws of Congress in respect to those matters do not extend into the territorial limits of the States, but have force only in the District of Columbia, and other places that are within the exclusive jurisdiction of the national government.[73]

---

[70] "The federal and State governments are in fact but different agents and trustees of the people, constituted with different powers and designed for different purposes.... [T]he ultimate authority, wherever the derivative may be found, resides in the people alone," *The Federalist* No. 46, at 294 (James Madison) (Clinton Rossiter ed., 1961).

[71] "Here, in strictness, the people surrender nothing; and as they retain everything they have no need of particular reservations," *The Federalist* No. 84, at 513 (Alexander Hamilton) (Clinton Rossiter ed., 1961).

[72] U.S. Const. art. IV, § 3, cl. 2.

[73] *Caha v. United States*, 152 U.S. 211, 215 (1894).

Notwithstanding the moment, the commerce clause,[74] the 14th Amendment or other constitutional specification, "a state has the same undeniable and unlimited jurisdiction over all persons and things, within its territorial limits, as any foreign nation; where that jurisdiction is not surrendered or restrained by the Constitution of the United States[,]" and "all those powers which relate to merely municipal legislation, or what may, perhaps, more properly be called *internal police*, are not thus surrendered or restrained...."[75] As a matter of law throughout the Union, it is the State, not the United States, which is presumably sovereign.[76]

> The very highest duty of the States, when they entered into the Union under the Constitution, was to protect all persons within their boundaries in the enjoyment of these "unalienable rights with which they were endowed by their Creator." Sovereignty, for this purpose, rests alone with the States.[77]

---

[74] U.S. Const. art. I, § 8, cl. 3. In fact, "the 'power to regulate commerce among the several States'...was intended as a negative and preventive provision against injustice among the States themselves, rather than as a power to be used for the positive purposes of the General government, in which alone, however, the remedial power could be lodged." 3 Max Farrand, *The Records of the Federal Convention of 1787* 478 (James Madison) (1911).

[75] *New York v. Miln*, 36 U.S. 102, 139 (1837).

[76] "'All legislation is prima facie territorial.'" *American Banana Co. v. United Fruit Co.*, 213 U.S. 347, 357 (1909) (quoting *Ex parte Blain*, L.R. 12 Ch.Div. 522, 528; *State v. Carter*, 27 N.J.L. 499; *People v. Merrill*, 2 Parker, Crim.Rep. 590, 596). "Legislation is presumptively territorial, and confined to limits over which the lawmaking power has jurisdiction." *Sandberg v. McDonald*, 248 U.S. 185, 195 (1918).

[77] *United States v. Cruikshank*, 92 U.S. 542, 553 (1875). *See also* Abraham Lincoln, *The Gettysburg Address* para. 1 (November 19, 1863).

Ratification altered the legal build of the United States by creating a national authority to act *under* the Union.[78] The Constitution changed the original structure of the United States "from a form merely federal" during the Articles of Confederation "to one partly national," though under similar limitations.[79]

> Federalism was our Nation's own discovery. The Framers split the atom of sovereignty. It was the genius of their idea that our citizens would have two political capacities, one state and one federal, each protected from incursion by the other. The resulting Constitution created a legal system unprecedented in form and design, establishing two orders of government, each with its own direct relationship, its own privity, its own set of mutual rights and obligations to the people who sustain it and are governed by it. It is appropriate to recall these origins, which instruct us as to the nature of the two different governments created and confirmed by the Constitution.[80]

---

[78] United States legislative power over the seat of national business is collocated with the other federal powers in Article 1, section 8 of the Constitution; clause 17 "granted an exclusive authority to the Union...." *The Federalist* No. 32, at 198 (Alexander Hamilton) (Clinton Rossiter ed., 1961).

[79] 3 Max Farrand, *The Records of the Federal Convention of 1787* 484 (James Madison) (1911). In either instance the general terms prefixed to the enumerated powers are limitative rather than expansive, *id.* The term *national* as contradistinguished from the term *federal* "was not meant to express the *extent* of power, but the *mode* of *its operation*," 3 *id.* at 474.

[80] *U.S. Term Limits, Inc. v. Thornton*, 514 U.S. 779, 838-839 (1995) (Kennedy, J., concurring).

The end result was "the perfection of the *system*"[81] rather than the outright perfection of the Union, thereby "distinguishing it from a plenary & Consolidated Govt."[82]

> The proposed Constitution, so far from implying an abolition of the State governments, makes them constituent parts of the national sovereignty...and leaves in their possession certain exclusive and very important portions of sovereign power. This fully corresponds, in every rational import of the terms, with the idea of a federal government.[83]

> An entire consolidation of the States into one complete national sovereignty would imply an entire subordination of the parts; and whatever powers might remain in them would be altogether dependent on the general will. But as the plan of the convention aims only at a partial union or consolidation, the State governments would clearly retain all the rights of sovereignty which they before had, and which were not, by that act, *exclusively* delegated to the United States.[84]

---

[81] *The Federalist* No. 80, at 481 (Alexander Hamilton) (Clinton Rossiter ed., 1961) (emphasis added).

[82] 3 Max Farrand, *The Records of the Federal Convention of 1787* 517 (James Madison) (1911).

[83] *The Federalist* No. 9, at 76 (Alexander Hamilton) (Clinton Rossiter ed., 1961).

[84] *The Federalist* No. 32, at 198 (Alexander Hamilton) (Clinton Rossiter ed., 1961).

The United States of America were never organized by a national government completely sovereign at the top over provinces, districts or states serving merely as "subordinate corporations" of the national state.[85]

---

[85] *Chisholm v. Georgia*, 2 U.S. 419, 448 (1793) (opinion of Iredell, J.). "The plan of the convention declares that the power of Congress, or, in other words, of the *national legislature*, shall extend to certain enumerated cases. This specification of particulars evidently excludes all pretension to a general legislative authority, because an affirmative grant of special powers would be absurd as well as useless if a general authority was intended." *The Federalist* No. 83, at 497 (Alexander Hamilton) (Clinton Rossiter ed., 1961). "And that the language of our Constitution is already undergoing interpretations unknown to its founders will, I believe, appear to all unbiased inquirers into the history of its origin and adoption." 3 Max Farrand, *The Records of the Federal Convention of 1787* 464 (James Madison) (1911). "Will you pardon me for pointing out an error of fact into which you have fallen, as others have done, by supposing that the term, *national* applied to the contemplated Government, in the early stage of the Convention...was equivalent to *unlimited* or consolidated. This was not the case. The term was used, not in contradistinction to a limited, but to a *federal* Government." 3 *id.* at 473. "And there being no technical or appropriate denomination applicable to the new and unique System, the term national was used, with a confidence that it would not be taken in a wrong sense, especially as a right one could be readily suggested if not sufficiently implied by some of the propositions themselves." 3 *id.* "It ought to have occurred that the Govt. of the U.S. being a novelty & a compound, had no technical terms or phrases appropriate to it; and that old terms were to be used in new senses, explained by the context or by the facts of the case." 3 *id.* at 517. "[T]he real character of the Govt. was & is obvious; this being necessarily deduced from the actual structure of the Govt. and the quantum of its powers." 3 *id.* at 517-518. "As the System was to be a new & compound one a nondescript without a technical appellation for it, the term 'National' was very naturally suggested by its national features." 3 *id.* at 529. "But what alone would justify & acct. for the application of the term National to the proposed Govt. is that it wd. possess, exclusively all the attributes of a natl. Govt. in its relations with other nations.... A Govt: which alone is known & acknowledged by all foreign nations, and alone charged with the international relations, could not fail to be deemed & called at home, a Natl. Govt." 3 *id.* at 529-530.

In America, the national and state governments are separate jurisdictions having no common superior except the people, however prevalent the misperception may be that the Supremacy Clause of the Constitution somehow makes legislation of Congress per se, even treaties per se, "the supreme Law of the Land."[86]

Forensically, of course, *"this Constitution"* and laws express the absolute rule.[87] The sovereign text by its own terms is the supreme law of the land, emanating from the people, the repository of ultimate sovereignty under our form of government. It is by the hand of the people that the individual States are "no more subject, within their respective spheres, to the general authority than the general authority is subject to them, within its own sphere."[88] Bear in mind a combination of incomplete governments yielding one complete system of American jurisprudence: "This separation of the two spheres is one of the Constitution's structural protections of liberty."[89]

The State governments and the National government all have functions and an expression of sovereignty within a unique *federal system*, which has been termed "Our Federalism." "It should never be forgotten that this slogan, 'Our Federalism,' born in the early struggling days of our Union of States, occupies a highly important place in our Nation's history and its future."[90]

---

[86] U.S. Const. art. VI, cl. 2.

[87] "It will not, I presume, have escaped observation that it *expressly* confines this supremacy to laws made *pursuant to the Constitution....*" *The Federalist* No. 34, at 205 (Alexander Hamilton) (Clinton Rossiter ed., 1961).

[88] *The Federalist* No. 39, at 245 (James Madison) (Clinton Rossiter ed., 1961).

[89] *Printz v. United States*, 521 U.S. 898, 921 (1997).

[90] *Younger v. Harris*, 401 U.S. 37, 44-45 (1971).

What emerged from this struggle was a new kind of federal system with a new kind of national government operating in a limited way among otherwise sovereign states. See *United States Reports* Vol. 92 for the record:

We have in our political system a government of the United States and a government of each of the several States. Each one of these governments is distinct from the others, and each has citizens of its own who owe it allegiance, and whose rights, within its jurisdiction, it must protect. The same person may be at the same time a citizen of the United States and a citizen of a State, but his rights of citizenship under one of these governments will be different from those he has under the other.

Experience made the fact known to the people of the United States that they required a national government for national purposes.... [They] ordained and established the government of the United States, and defined its powers by a constitution, which they adopted as its fundamental law, and made its rule of action.

The government thus established and defined is to some extent a government of the States in their political capacity. It is also, for certain purposes, a government of the people. Its powers are limited in number, but not in degree. Within the scope of its powers, as enumerated and defined, it is supreme and above the States; but beyond, it has no existence.

The people of the United States resident within any State are subject to two governments: one State, and the other National; but there need be no conflict between the two. The powers which one possesses, the other does not. They are established for different purposes, and have separate jurisdictions. Together they make one whole, and furnish the people of the United States with a complete government, ample for the protection of all their rights at home and abroad.[91]

Fifty states "at home" and one United States "abroad" complement a system[92] to protect the country on all sides: national powers "will be exercised principally on external objects," while "powers reserved to the several states will extend to all the objects which, in the ordinary course of affairs, concern the lives, liberties, and properties of the people, and the internal order, improvement, and prosperity of the State."[93] America's local jurisdictions and individuals have the preponderance of dominion and autonomy.

The general idea is that the several States still retain "all *internal sovereignty*" while the United States possess "the great *rights of external sovereignty*[.]"[94]

---

[91] *United States v. Cruikshank*, 92 U.S. 542, 549-550 (1875).

[92] The national and state governments truly are "parts of ONE WHOLE," *The Federalist* No. 82, at 493 (Alexander Hamilton) (Clinton Rossiter ed., 1961).

[93] *The Federalist* No. 45, at 292-293 (James Madison) (Clinton Rossiter ed., 1961).

[94] *Ware v. Hylton*, 3 U.S. 199, 232 (1796).

The Constitution lays down the principles of limited government.[95] Already vested with land and law inside their States, the people of the Union chose to project a United States government predominant along state lines, and denied to their nation "an indefinite supremacy over all persons and things," even "so far as they are objects of lawful government."[96]

Objectionably, our United States devolve into a general municipal authority broadly exercising the type of inland jurisdiction that appropriately squares with the seat of the government. This brand of United States, nominally federal, instead takes on the loose contours of a brooding national superstate elaborating on equity and commercial suasion rather than law in the ordinary sense.[97]

---

[95] As conceived, "this is not an indefinite Government, deriving its powers from the general terms prefixed to the specified powers, but a limited Government, tied down to the specified powers which explain and define the general terms." 3 Max Farrand, *The Records of the Federal Convention of 1787* 366 (James Madison) (1911). "For what purpose could the enumeration of particular powers be inserted, if these and all others were meant to be included in the preceding general power?" *The Federalist* No. 41, at 263 (James Madison) (Clinton Rossiter ed., 1961).

[96] *The Federalist* No. 39, at 245 (James Madison) (Clinton Rossiter ed., 1961). "In the first place it is to be remembered that the general government is not to be charged with the whole power of making and administering laws. Its jurisdiction is limited to certain enumerated objects," *The Federalist* No. 14, *id.* at 102 (James Madison).

[97] "The operations of the national government, on the other hand, falling less immediately under the observation of the mass of the citizens, the benefits derived from it will chiefly be perceived and attended to by speculative men." *The Federalist* No. 17, at 120 (Alexander Hamilton) (Clinton Rossiter ed., 1961). "Every new regulation concerning commerce or revenue, or in any manner affecting the value of the different species of property, presents a new harvest to those who watch the change, and can trace it consequences...." *The Federalist* No. 62, at 380 (James Madison) (Clinton Rossiter ed., 1961).

Our Constitution is a legal agreement between and among *We the People of the United States*, and the words "general" and "perfect" are law words, with law meanings, as real as the differences between federal United States and a national United States.

Today, even keeping to a vague preambular authority "to promote the general welfare" would serve to restrict, rather than extend, national governance, insofar as any "general" law by definition applies everywhere *and only everywhere*, to everyone *and only everyone*, without discrimination or suspense. Yet few congressional acts are made to apply generally throughout the United States. Provisions take hold here and there, but not everywhere, even to laws of crime.[98] These intermittent federal zones defy the general nature of United States power and cross geographic stopping points put in place by the people.[99]

Certainly Americans have a right to "come to the seat of government[.]"[100] It is, after all, our national territory. But the Constitution distinguishes incidents within and without State territory, where residence attaches the most fundamental rights to a citizen.[101]

---

[98] *United States v. Lopez*, 514 U.S. 549 (1995). "The tendency of this statute to displace state regulation in areas of traditional state concern is evident from its territorial operation." *Id.* at 583 (Kennedy, J., concurring).
[99] U.S. Const. art. I, § 8, cl. 17. U.S. Const. art. IV, § 3, cl. 2.
[100] *Slaughterhouse Cases*, 83 U.S. 36, 79 (1873).
[101] "It may be esteemed the basis of the Union that 'the citizens of each State shall be entitled to all the privileges and immunities of citizens of the several States.'" *The Federalist* No. 80, at 478 (Alexander Hamilton) (Clinton Rossiter ed., 1961). U.S. Const. art. IV, § 2, cl. 1. In keeping with the purposes of the Union and the legal equality of its citizens, this clause offers no rights or protections within the District of Columbia, territories and possessions -- only within the States.

Close

Our courts uphold the first sovereignty of the people, without which the supremacy of the Constitution becomes merely ideal.[102]

Before the Declaration of Independence this concept *was* speculative; but that document advanced the ideas of legal equality and popular sovereignty that came together in the United States Constitution, and the subordination of all powers to law. *The theory of our political system is that the ultimate sovereignty is in the people, and by the constitutions which they form, not even the whole people as an aggregate body are free to take action against these fundamental laws, having set limits upon the extent and mode of law-making even by themselves.*[103]

This is to say that the Constitution secures our basic freedoms by precluding a national electorate, which may alter or abolish the very government itself.[104] Ours is a permanent Constitution. The common law informs its construction, and Americans understand it as higher law.

---

[102] Judges "are to be the interpreters of the law," *The Federalist* No. 73, at 446 (Alexander Hamilton) (Clinton Rossiter ed., 1961). "Laws are a dead letter without courts to expound and define their true meaning and operation." *The Federalist* No. 22, *id.* at 150 (Alexander Hamilton).

[103] Thomas M. Cooley, *Constitutional Limitations* 33 (6th Ed. 1890). James DeWitt Andrews, *American Law and Procedure* Vol. XIII, *Jurisprudence and Legal Institutions* 263 (1913). Our national collective is not identified as a body politic for any legal or constitutional purpose; this means *"the total exclusion of the people in their collective capacity"* from any share in the system. *The Federalist* No. 63, at 387 (James Madison) (Clinton Rossiter ed., 1961).

[104] "One's right to life, liberty, and property, to free speech, a free press, freedom of worship and assembly, and other fundamental rights may not be submitted to vote; they depend on the outcome of no elections." *West Virginia State Board of Education v. Barnette*, 319 U.S. 624, 638 (1943).

The people made the Constitution by way of their States and may convene there to amend it.[105] The government created by it is not formed or reorganized when we vote. No election can derange it. Perhaps its best source of public confidence and respect is this constancy.[106] Our government has never "fallen" because the people of the United States, rather than confide their sovereignty to each other at the ballot box, put it down in writing in the form of fundamental law in a compact draft, creating a "government of laws, and not of men."[107]

People trust the Constitution because they understand it, as they basically understand their common ground.[108]

The press of money and power may disserve the law; arcane legal rulings may even circumvent its application; occulted legislation may lurk about; but all must answer at last to the plain terms of the Constitution.[109]

---

[105] U.S. Const. Art. V. "In opposition to the probability of subsequent amendments, it has been urged that the persons delegated to the administration of the national government will always be disinclined to yield up any portion of the authority of which they were once possessed." *The Federalist* No. 85, at 525 (Alexander Hamilton) (Clinton Rossiter ed., 1961). However, the national rulers are given "no option upon the subject." *Id.* at 526. "Nothing in this particular is left to the discretion of [the Congress]." *Id.*

[106] "The Constitution is a written instrument. As such its meaning does not alter." *South Carolina v. United States*, 199 U.S. 437, 448 (1905).

[107] C. Bradley Thompson, *The Revolutionary Writings of John Adams* 226 (2000). Adams defines a *republic*, advancing the governmental form guaranteed to every State by the Constitution. U.S. Const. art. IV, § 4.

[108] Whereas "rules of legal interpretation are rules of *common sense*," *The Federalist* No. 83, at 496 (Alexander Hamilton) (Clinton Rossiter ed., 1961), the Constitution is not subject to private interpretation.

[109] Admittedly, "the Constitution ought to be the standard of construction for the laws," so that "wherever there is an evident opposition, the laws ought to give place to the Constitution." *The Federalist* No. 81, at 482 (Alexander Hamilton) (Clinton Rossiter ed., 1961).

No other nation on earth has realized the self-control to establish this order of freedom, to set high law against "the mischievous effects of a mutable government[.]"[110]

> [A] very large Field presents to our view without a single Straight or eligible Road that has been trodden by the feet of nations. An Union of Sovereign States, preserving their Civil Liberties and connected together by such Tyes as to Preserve permanent & efective Governments is a system not described, it is a Circumstance that has not Occurred in the History of men; if we shall be so fortunate as to find this in descript our Time will have been well spent.[111]

Thanks to our common-law ground, the plural nature of our Union, and certain distinctive technical features built-in to the Constitution of the United States at least one determination holds true: the United States really are a free country.

---

[110] *The Federalist* No. 62, at 380 (James Madison) (Clinton Rossiter ed., 1961). "It will be of little avail to the people that the laws are made by men of their own choice if the laws be so voluminous that they cannot be read, or so incoherent that they cannot be understood; if they be repealed or revised before they are promulgated, or undergo such incessant changes that no man, who knows what the law is today, can guess what it will be tomorrow. Law is defined to be a rule of action; but how can that be a rule, which is little known, and less fixed?" *Id*. at 381.
[111] 3 Max Farrand, *The Records of the Federal Convention of 1787* 46 (North Carolina Delegates) (1911).

IN CONGRESS, July 4, 1776.

The unanimous Declaration of the thirteen united States of America,

When in the Course of human events, it becomes necessary for one people to dissolve the political bands which have connected them with another, and to assume among the powers of the earth, the separate and equal station to which the Laws of Nature and of Nature's God entitle them, a decent respect to the opinions of mankind requires that they should declare the causes which impel them to the separation.

—We hold these truths to be self-evident, that all men are created equal, that they are endowed by their Creator with certain unalienable Rights, that among these are Life, Liberty and the pursuit of Happiness. —That to secure these rights, Governments are instituted among Men, deriving their just powers from the consent of the governed, —That whenever any Form of Government becomes destructive of these ends, it is the Right of the People to alter or to abolish it, and to institute new Government, laying its foundation on such principles and organizing its powers in such form, as to them shall seem most likely to effect their Safety and Happiness. Prudence, indeed, will dictate that Governments long established should not be changed for light and transient causes; and accordingly all experience hath shewn, that mankind are more disposed to suffer, while evils are sufferable, than to right themselves by abolishing the forms to which they are accustomed. But when a long train of abuses and usurpations, pursuing invariably the same Object evinces a design to reduce them under absolute Despotism, it is their right, it is their duty, to throw off such Government, and to provide new Guards for their future security. —Such has been the patient sufferance of these Colonies; and such is now the necessity which constrains them to alter their former Systems of Government. The history of the present King of Great Britain is a history of repeated injuries and usurpations, all having in direct object the establishment of an absolute Tyranny over these States. To prove this, let Facts be submitted to a candid world.

—He has refused his Assent to Laws, the most wholesome and necessary for the public good.

—He has forbidden his Governors to pass Laws of immediate and pressing importance, unless suspended in their operation till his Assent should be obtained; and when so suspended, he has utterly neglected to attend to them.

—He has refused to pass other Laws for the accommodation of large districts of people, unless those people would relinquish the right of Representation in the Legislature, a right inestimable to them and formidable to tyrants only.

—He has called together legislative bodies at places unusual, uncomfortable, and distant from the depository of their public Records, for the sole purpose of fatiguing them into compliance with his measures.

—He has dissolved Representative Houses repeatedly, for opposing with manly firmness his invasions on the rights of the people.

—He has refused for a long time, after such dissolutions, to cause others to be elected; whereby the Legislative powers, incapable of Annihilation, have returned to the People at large for their exercise;

the State remaining in the mean time exposed to all the dangers of invasion from without, and convulsions within.

—He has endeavoured to prevent the population of these States; for that purpose obstructing the Laws for Naturalization of Foreigners; refusing to pass others to encourage their migrations hither, and raising the conditions of new Appropriations of Lands.

—He has obstructed the Administration of Justice, by refusing his Assent to Laws for establishing Judiciary powers.

—He has made Judges dependent on his Will alone, for the tenure of their offices, and the amount and payment of their salaries.

—He has erected a multitude of New Offices, and sent hither swarms of Officers to harrass our people, and eat out their substance.

—He has kept among us, in times of peace, Standing Armies without the Consent of our legislatures.

—He has affected to render the Military independent of and superior to the Civil power.

—He has combined with others to subject us to a jurisdiction foreign to our constitution, and unacknowledged by our laws; giving his Assent to their Acts of pretended Legislation:

—For Quartering large bodies of armed troops among us:

—For protecting them, by a mock Trial, from punishment for any Murders which they should commit on the Inhabitants of these States:

—For cutting off our Trade with all parts of the world:

—For imposing Taxes on us without our Consent:

—For depriving us in many cases, of the benefits of Trial by Jury:

—For transporting us beyond Seas to be tried for pretended offences

—For abolishing the free System of English Laws in a neighbouring Province, establishing therein an Arbitrary government, and enlarging its Boundaries so as to render it at once an example and fit instrument for introducing the same absolute rule into these Colonies:

—For taking away our Charters, abolishing our most valuable Laws, and altering fundamentally the Forms of our Governments:

—For suspending our own Legislatures, and declaring themselves invested with power to legislate for us in all cases whatsoever.

—He has abdicated Government here, by declaring us out of his Protection and waging War against us.

—He has plundered our seas, ravaged our Coasts, burnt our towns, and destroyed the lives of our people.

—He is at this time transporting large Armies of foreign Mercenaries to compleat the works of death, desolation and tyranny, already begun with circumstances of Cruelty & perfidy scarcely paralleled in the most barbarous ages, and totally unworthy the Head of a civilized nation.

—He has constrained our fellow Citizens taken Captive on the high Seas to bear Arms against their Country, to become the executioners of their friends and Brethren, or to fall themselves by their Hands.

—He has excited domestic insurrections amongst us, and has endeavoured to bring on the inhabitants of our frontiers, the merciless Indian Savages, whose known rule of warfare, is an undistinguished destruction of all ages, sexes and conditions.

In every stage of these Oppressions We have Petitioned for Redress in the most humble terms: Our repeated Petitions have been answered only by repeated injury. A Prince whose character is thus marked by every act which may define a Tyrant, is unfit to be the ruler of a free people.

Nor have We been wanting in attentions to our Brittish brethren. We have warned them from time to time of attempts by their legislature to extend an unwarrantable jurisdiction over us. We have reminded them of the circumstances of our emigration and settlement here. We have appealed to their native justice and magnanimity, and we have conjured them by the ties of our common kindred to disavow these usurpations, which, would inevitably interrupt our connections and correspondence. They too have been deaf to the voice of justice and of consanguinity. We must, therefore, acquiesce in the necessity, which denounces our Separation, and hold them, as we hold the rest of mankind, Enemies in War, in Peace Friends.

We, therefore, the Representatives of the united States of America, in General Congress, Assembled, appealing to the Supreme Judge of the world for the rectitude of our intentions, do, in the Name, and by Authority of the good People of these Colonies, solemnly publish and declare, That these United Colonies are, and of Right ought to be Free and Independent States; that they are Absolved from all Allegiance to the British Crown, and that all political connection between them and the State of Great Britain, is and ought to be totally dissolved; and that as Free and Independent States, they have full Power to levy War, conclude Peace, contract Alliances, establish Commerce, and to do all other Acts and Things which Independent States may of right do. And for the support of this Declaration, with a firm reliance on the protection of divine Providence, we mutually pledge to each other our Lives, our Fortunes and our sacred Honor.

Button Gwinnett	Caesar Rodney
Lyman Hall	George Read
George Walton	Thomas McKean
William Hooper	William Floyd
Joseph Hewes	Philip Livingston
John Penn	Francis Lewis
Edward Rutledge	Lewis Morris
Thomas Heyward, Jr.	Richard Stockton
Thomas Lynch, Jr.	John Witherspoon
Arthur Middleton	Francis Hopkinson
John Hancock	John Hart
Samuel Chase	Abraham Clark
William Paca	Josiah Bartlett
Thomas Stone	William Whipple
Charles Carroll of Carrollton	Samuel Adams
George Wythe	John Adams
Richard Henry Lee	Robert Treat Paine
Thomas Jefferson	Elbridge Gerry
Benjamin Harrison	Stephen Hopkins
Thomas Nelson, Jr.	William Ellery
Francis Lightfoot Lee	Roger Sherman
Carter Braxton	Samuel Huntington
Robert Morris	William Williams
Benjamin Rush	Oliver Wolcott
Benjamin Franklin	Matthew Thornton
John Morton	George Clymer
James Smith	George Taylor
James Wilson	George Ross

To all to whom these Presents shall come, we the undersigned Delegates of the States affixed to our Names send greeting.

Whereas the Delegates of the United States of America in Congress assembled, did on the fifteenth day of November, in the year of our Lord one thousand seven hundred and seventy-seven, and in the second year of the Independence of America, agree to certain articles of Confederation and perpetual Union between the states of New Hampshire, Massachusetts Bay, Rhode Island and Providence Plantations, Connecticut, New York, New Jersey, Pennsylvania, Delaware, Maryland, Virginia, North Carolina, South Carolina, and Georgia, in the words following, viz.

Articles of Confederation and perpetual Union between the States of New Hampshire, Massachusetts-bay, Rhode Island and Providence Plantations, Connecticut, New York, New Jersey, Pennsylvania, Delaware, Maryland, Virginia, North Carolina, South Carolina and Georgia.

Article I. The Stile of this Confederacy shall be "The United States of America".

Article II. Each State retains its sovereignty, freedom, and independence, and every power, jurisdiction, and right, which is not by this confederation expressly delegated to the United States, in Congress assembled.

Article III. The said States hereby severally enter into a firm league of friendship with each other, for their common defense, the security of their liberties, and their mutual and general welfare, binding themselves to assist each other, against all force offered to, or attacks made upon them, or any of them, on account of religion, sovereignty, trade, or any other pretense whatever.

Article IV. The better to secure and perpetuate mutual friendship and intercourse among the people of the different States in this union, the free inhabitants of each of these States, paupers, vagabonds, and fugitives from justice excepted, shall be entitled to all privileges and immunities of free citizens in the several States; and the people of each State shall have free ingress and regress to and from any other State, and shall enjoy therein all the privileges of trade and commerce, subject to the same duties, impositions, and restrictions as the inhabitants thereof respectively, provided that such restrictions shall not extend so far as to prevent the removal of property imported into any State, to any other State of which the owner is an inhabitant; provided also that no imposition, duties or restriction shall be laid by any State, on the property of the united States, or either of them.

If any person guilty of, or charged with, treason, felony, or other high misdemeanor in any State, shall flee from justice, and be found in any of the united States, he shall, upon demand of the Governor or executive power of the State from which he fled, be delivered up and removed to the State having jurisdiction of his offense.

Full faith and credit shall be given in each of these States to the records, acts, and judicial proceedings of the courts and magistrates of every other State.

Article V. For the most convenient management of the general interests of the united States, delegates shall be annually appointed in such manner as the legislatures of each State shall direct, to meet in congress on the first Monday in November, in every year, with a power reserved to each State to recall its delegates, or any of them, at any time within the year, and to send others in their stead for the remainder of the year.

No State shall be represented in congress by less than two, nor more than seven members; and no person shall be capable of being a delegate for more than three years in any term of six years; nor shall any person, being a delegate, be capable of holding any office under the united States, for which he, or another for his benefit, receives any salary, fees or emolument of any kind.

Each State shall maintain its own delegates in a meeting of the States, and while they act as members of the committee of the States.

In determining questions in the united States, in Congress assembled, each State shall have one vote.

Freedom of speech and debate in Congress shall not be impeached or questioned in any Court or place out of Congress, and the members of congress shall be protected in their persons from arrests or imprisonments, during the time of their going to and from, and attendence on congress, except for treason, felony, or breach of the peace.

Article VI. No State, without the consent of the united States in congress assembled, shall send any embassy to, or receive any embassy from, or enter into any conference, agreement, alliance or treaty with any King, Prince or State; nor shall any person holding any office of profit or trust under the united States, or any of them, accept any present, emolument, office or title of any kind whatever from any King, Prince or foreign State; nor shall the united States in congress assembled, or any of them, grant any title of nobility.

No two or more States shall enter into any treaty, confederation or alliance whatever between them, without the consent of the united States in Congress assembled, specifying accurately the purposes for which the same is to be entered into, and how long it shall continue.

No State shall lay any imposts or duties, which may interfere with any stipulations in treaties, entered into by the united States in congress assembled, with any King, Prince or State, in pursuance of any treaties already proposed by congress, to the courts of France and Spain.

No vessel of war shall be kept up in time of peace by any State, except such number only, as shall be deemed necessary by the united States in congress assembled, for the defense of such State, or its trade; nor shall any body of forces be kept up by any State in time of peace, except such number only, as in the judgement of the united States in congress assembled, shall be deemed requisite to garrison the forts necessary for the defense of such State; but every State shall always keep up a well-regulated and disciplined militia, sufficiently armed and accoutered, and shall provide and constantly have ready for use, in public stores, a due number of field pieces and tents, and a proper quantity of arms, ammunition and camp equipage.

No State shall engage in any war without the consent of the united States in congress assembled, unless such State be actually invaded by enemies, or shall have received certain advice of a resolution being formed by some nation of Indians to invade such State, and the danger is so imminent as not to admit of a delay till the united States in congress assembled can be consulted; nor shall any State grant commissions to any ships or vessels of war, nor letters of marque or reprisal, except it be after a declaration of war by the united States in congress assembled, and then only against the Kingdom or State and the subjects thereof, against which war has been so declared, and under such regulations as shall be established by the united States in congress assembled, unless such State be infested by pirates, in which case vessels of war may be fitted out for that occasion, and kept so long as the danger shall continue, or until the united States in congress assembled shall determine otherwise.

Article VII. When land forces are raised by any State for the common defense, all officers of or under the rank of colonel, shall be appointed by the legislature of each State respectively, by whom such forces shall be raised, or in such manner as such State shall direct, and all vacancies shall be filled up by the State which first made the appointment.

Article VIII. All charges of war, and all other expenses that shall be incurred for the common defense or general welfare, and allowed by the united States in Congress assembled, shall be defrayed out of a common treasury, which shall be supplied by the several States in proportion to the value of all land within each State, granted or surveyed for any person, as such land and the buildings and improvements thereon shall be estimated according to such mode as the united States in Congress assembled, shall from time to time direct and appoint.

The taxes for paying that proportion shall be laid and levied by the authority and direction of the legislatures of the several States within the time agreed upon by the united States in congress assembled.

Article IX. The united States in congress assembled, shall have the sole and exclusive right and power of determining on peace and war, except in the cases mentioned in the sixth article — of sending and receiving ambassadors — entering into treaties and alliances, provided that no treaty of commerce shall be made whereby the legislative power of the respective States shall be restrained from imposing such imposts and duties on foreigners, as their own people are subjected to, or from prohibiting the exportation or importation of any species of goods or commodities whatsoever — of establishing rules for deciding in all cases, what captures on land or water shall be legal, and in what manner prizes taken by land or naval forces in the service of the united States shall be divided or appropriated — of granting letters of marque and reprisal in times of peace — appointing courts for the trial of piracies and felonies commited on the high seas and establishing courts for receiving and determining finally appeals in all cases of captures, provided that no member of congress shall be appointed a judge of any of the said courts.

The united States in congress assembled shall also be the last resort on appeal in all disputes and differences now subsisting or that hereafter may arise between two or more States concerning boundary, jurisdiction or any other causes whatever; which authority shall always be exercised in the manner following. Whenever the legislative or executive authority or lawful agent of any State in controversy with another shall present a petition to congress stating the matter in question and praying for a hearing, notice thereof shall be given by order of congress to the legislative or executive authority of the other State in controversy, and a day assigned for the appearance of the parties by their lawful agents, who shall then be directed to appoint by joint consent, commissioners or judges to constitute a court for hearing and determining the matter in question: but if they cannot agree, congress shall name three persons out of each of the united States, and from the list of such persons each party shall alternately strike out one, the petitioners beginning, until the number shall be reduced to thirteen; and from that number not less than seven, nor more than nine names as congress shall direct, shall in the presence of congress be drawn out by lot, and the persons whose names shall be so drawn or any five of them, shall be commissioners or judges, to hear and finally determine the controversy, so always as a major part of the judges who shall hear the cause shall agree in the determination: and if either party shall neglect to attend at the day appointed, without showing reasons, which congress shall judge sufficient, or being present shall refuse to strike, the congress shall proceed to nominate three persons out of each State, and the secretary of congress shall strike in behalf of such party absent or refusing; and the judgement and sentence of the court to be appointed, in the manner before prescribed, shall be final and conclusive; and if any of the parties shall refuse to submit to the authority of such court, or to appear or defend their claim or cause, the court shall nevertheless proceed to pronounce sentence, or judgement, which shall in like manner be final and decisive, the judgement or sentence and other proceedings being in either case transmitted to congress, and lodged among the acts of congress for the security of the parties concerned: provided that every commissioner, before he sits in judgement, shall take an oath to be administered by one of the judges of the supreme or superior court of the State, where the cause shall be tried, 'well and truly to hear and determine the matter in question, according to the best of his judgement, without favor, affection or hope of reward': provided also, that no State shall be deprived of territory for the benefit of the united States.

All controversies concerning the private right of soil claimed under different grants of two or more States, whose jurisdictions as they may respect such lands, and the States which passed such grants are adjusted, the said grants or either of them being at the same time claimed to have originated antecedent to such settlement of jurisdiction, shall on the petition of either party to the congress of the united States, be finally determined as near as may be in the same manner as is before prescribed for deciding disputes respecting territorial jurisdiction between different States.

The united States in congress assembled shall also have the sole and exclusive right and power of regulating the alloy and value of coin struck by their own authority, or by that of the respective States — fixing the standards of weights and measures throughout the united States — regulating the trade and managing all affairs with the Indians, not members of any of the States, provided that the legislative right of any State within its own limits be not infringed or violated — establishing and regulating post-offices from one State to another, throughout all the united States, and exacting such postage on the papers passing through the same as may be requisite to defray the expenses of the said office — appointing all officers of the land forces, in the service of the united States, excepting regimental officers — appointing all the officers of the naval forces, and commissioning all officers whatever in the service of the united States —

making rules for the government and regulation of the said land and naval forces, and directing their operations.

The united States in congress assembled shall have authority to appoint a committee, to sit in the recess of congress, to be denominated 'A Committee of the States', and to consist of one delegate from each State; and to appoint such other committees and civil officers as may be necessary for managing the general affairs of the united States under their direction — to appoint one of their members to preside, provided that no person be allowed to serve in the office of president more than one year in any term of three years; to ascertain the necessary sums of money to be raised for the service of the united States, and to appropriate and apply the same for defraying the public expenses — to borrow money, or emit bills on the credit of the united States, transmitting every half-year to the respective States an account of the sums of money so borrowed or emitted — to build and equip a navy — to agree upon the number of land forces, and to make requisitions from each State for its quota, in proportion to the number of white inhabitants in such State; which requisition shall be binding, and thereupon the legislature of each State shall appoint the regimental officers, raise the men and cloath, arm and equip them in a soldier-like manner, at the expense of the united States; and the officers and men so cloathed, armed and equipped shall march to the place appointed, and within the time agreed on by the united States in congress assembled. But if the united States in congress assembled shall, on consideration of circumstances judge proper that any State should not raise men, or should raise a smaller number of men than the quota thereof, such extra number shall be raised, officered, cloathed, armed and equipped in the same manner as the quota of each State, unless the legislature of such State shall judge that such extra number cannot be safely spared out of the same, in which case they shall raise, officer, cloath, arm and equip as many of such extra number as they judge can be safely spared. And the officers and men so cloathed, armed, and equipped, shall march to the place appointed, and within the time agreed on by the united States in congress assembled.

The united States in congress assembled shall never engage in a war, nor grant letters of marque or reprisal in time of peace, nor enter into any treaties or alliances, nor coin money, nor regulate the value thereof, nor ascertain the sums and expenses necessary for the defense and welfare of the united States, or any of them, nor emit bills, nor borrow money on the credit of the united States, nor appropriate money, nor agree upon the number of vessels of war, to be built or purchased, or the number of land or sea forces to be raised, nor appoint a commander in chief of the army or navy, unless nine States assent to the same: nor shall a question on any other point, except for adjourning from day to day be determined, unless by the votes of the majority of the united States in congress assembled.

The congress of the united States shall have power to adjourn to any time within the year, and to any place within the united States, so that no period of adjournment be for a longer duration than the space of six months, and shall publish the journal of their proceedings monthly, except such parts thereof relating to treaties, alliances or military operations, as in their judgement require secrecy; and the yeas and nays of the delegates of each State on any question shall be entered on the journal, when it is desired by any delegates of a State, or any of them, at his or their request shall be furnished with a transcript of the said journal, except such parts as are above excepted, to lay before the legislatures of the several States.

Article X. The committee of the States, or any nine of them, shall be authorized to execute, in the recess of congress, such of the powers of congress as the United States in congress assembled, by the consent of the nine States, shall from time to time think expedient to vest them with; provided that no power be delegated to the said committee, for the exercise of which, by the articles of confederation, the voice of nine States in the congress of the united States assembled be requisite.

Article XI. Canada acceding to this confederation, and adjoining in the measures of the united States, shall be admitted into, and entitled to all the advantages of this union; but no other colony shall be admitted into the same, unless such admission be agreed to by nine States.

Article XII. All bills of credit emitted, monies borrowed, and debts contracted by, or under the authority of congress, before the assembling of the united States, in pursuance of the present confederation, shall be deemed and considered as a charge against the united States, for payment and satisfaction whereof the said united States, and the public faith are hereby solemnly pledged.

Article XIII. Every State shall abide by the determination of the united States in congress assembled, on all questions which by this confederation are submitted to them. And the Articles of this confederation shall be inviolably observed by every State, and the union shall be perpetual; nor shall any alteration at any time hereafter be made in any of them; unless such alteration be agreed to in a congress of the united States, and be afterwards confirmed by the legislatures of every State.

And Whereas it hath pleased the Great Governor of the World to incline the hearts of the legislatures we respectively represent in congress, to approve of, and to authorize us to ratify the said articles of confederation and perpetual union. **Know Ye** that we the undersigned delegates, by virtue of the power and authority to us given for that purpose, do by these presents, in the name and in behalf of our respective constituents, fully and entirely ratify and confirm each and every of the said articles of confederation and perpetual union, and all and singular the matters and things therein contained: And we do further solemnly plight and engage the faith of our respective constituents, that they shall abide by the determinations of the united States in congress assembled, on all questions, which by the said Confederation are submitted to them. And that the articles thereof shall be inviolably observed by the States we respectively represent, and that the Union shall be perpetual. In Witness whereof we have hereunto set our hands in Congress. Done at Philadelphia in the State of Pennsylvania the ninth day of July in the Year of our Lord One Thousand Seven Hundred and Seventy-Eight, and in the Third Year of the independence of America.

Agreed to by Congress 15 November 1777

In force after ratification by Maryland, 1 March 1781

We the People of the United States, in Order to form a more perfect Union, establish Justice, insure domestic Tranquility, provide for the common defence, promote the general Welfare, and secure the Blessings of Liberty to ourselves and our Posterity, do ordain and establish this Constitution for the United States of America.

Article. I.

Section. 1. All legislative Powers herein granted shall be vested in a Congress of the United States, which shall consist of a Senate and House of Representatives.

Section. 2. The House of Representatives shall be composed of Members chosen every second Year by the People of the several States, and the Electors in each State shall have the Qualifications requisite for Electors of the most numerous Branch of the State Legislature.

No Person shall be a Representative who shall not have attained to the Age of twenty five Years, and been seven Years a Citizen of the United States, and who shall not, when elected, be an Inhabitant of that State in which he shall be chosen.

Representatives and direct Taxes shall be apportioned among the several States which may be included within this Union, according to their respective Numbers, which shall be determined by adding to the whole Number of free Persons, including those bound to Service for a Term of Years, and excluding Indians not taxed, three fifths of all other Persons.[112] The actual Enumeration shall be made within three Years after the first Meeting of the Congress of the United States, and within every

---

[112] *See* Art. XIV.

subsequent Term of ten Years, in such Manner as they shall by Law direct. The Number of Representatives shall not exceed one for every thirty Thousand, but each State shall have at Least one Representative; and until such enumeration shall be made, the State of New Hampshire shall be entitled to chuse three, Massachusetts eight, Rhode-Island and Providence Plantations one, Connecticut five, New-York six, New Jersey four, Pennsylvania eight, Delaware one, Maryland six, Virginia ten, North Carolina five, South Carolina five, and Georgia three.

When vacancies happen in the Representation from any State, the Executive Authority thereof shall issue Writs of Election to fill such Vacancies.

The House of Representatives shall chuse their Speaker and other Officers; and shall have the sole Power of Impeachment.

Section. 3.   The Senate of the United States shall be composed of two Senators from each State, chosen by the Legislature thereof,[113] for six Years; and each Senator shall have one Vote.

Immediately after they shall be assembled in Consequence of the first Election, they shall be divided as equally as may be into three Classes. The Seats of the Senators of the first Class shall be vacated at the Expiration of the second Year, of the second Class at the Expiration of the fourth Year, and of the third Class at the Expiration of the sixth Year, so that one third may be chosen every second Year; and if Vacancies happen by Resignation, or otherwise, during the Recess of the Legislature of any State, the Executive thereof may make

---

[113] *See* Amend. XVII.

temporary Appointments until the next Meeting of the Legislature, which shall then fill such Vacancies.[114]

No Person shall be a Senator who shall not have attained to the Age of thirty Years, and been nine Years a Citizen of the United States, and who shall not, when elected, be an Inhabitant of that State for which he shall be chosen.

The Vice President of the United States shall be President of the Senate, but shall have no Vote, unless they be equally divided.

The Senate shall chuse their other Officers, and also a President pro tempore, in the Absence of the Vice President, or when he shall exercise the Office of President of the United States.

The Senate shall have the sole Power to try all Impeachments. When sitting for that Purpose, they shall be on Oath or Affirmation. When the President of the United States is tried, the Chief Justice shall preside: And no Person shall be convicted without the Concurrence of two thirds of the Members present.

Judgment in Cases of Impeachment shall not extend further than to removal from Office, and disqualification to hold and enjoy any Office of honor, Trust or Profit under the United States: but the Party convicted shall nevertheless be liable and subject to Indictment, Trial, Judgment and Punishment, according to Law.

Section. 4. The Times, Places and Manner of holding Elections for Senators and Representatives, shall be prescribed in each State by the Legislature thereof; but the Congress may at any time by Law make or alter such Regulations, except as to the Places of chusing Senators.

---

[114] *See* Amend. XVII.

The Congress shall assemble at least once in every Year, and such Meeting shall be on the first Monday in December,[115] unless they shall by Law appoint a different Day.

Section. 5. Each House shall be the Judge of the Elections, Returns and Qualifications of its own Members, and a Majority of each shall constitute a Quorum to do Business; but a smaller Number may adjourn from day to day, and may be authorized to compel the Attendance of absent Members, in such Manner, and under such Penalties as each House may provide.

Each House may determine the Rules of its Proceedings, punish its Members for disorderly Behaviour, and, with the Concurrence of two thirds, expel a Member.

Each House shall keep a Journal of its Proceedings, and from time to time publish the same, excepting such Parts as may in their Judgment require Secrecy; and the Yeas and Nays of the Members of either House on any question shall, at the Desire of one fifth of those Present, be entered on the Journal.

Neither House, during the Session of Congress, shall, without the Consent of the other, adjourn for more than three days, nor to any other Place than that in which the two Houses shall be sitting.

Section. 6. The Senators and Representatives shall receive a Compensation for their Services, to be ascertained by Law, and paid out of the Treasury of the United States. They shall in all Cases, except Treason, Felony and Breach of the Peace, be privileged from

---

[115] *See* Amend. XX.

Arrest during their Attendance at the Session of their respective Houses, and in going to and returning from the same; and for any Speech or Debate in either House, they shall not be questioned in any other Place.

No Senator or Representative shall, during the Time for which he was elected, be appointed to any civil Office under the Authority of the United States, which shall have been created, or the Emoluments whereof shall have been encreased during such time; and no Person holding any Office under the United States, shall be a Member of either House during his Continuance in Office.

Section. 7. All Bills for raising Revenue shall originate in the House of Representatives; but the Senate may propose or concur with Amendments as on other Bills.

Every Bill which shall have passed the House of Representatives and the Senate, shall, before it become a Law, be presented to the President of the United States: If he approve he shall sign it, but if not he shall return it, with his Objections to that House in which it shall have originated, who shall enter the Objections at large on their Journal, and proceed to reconsider it. If after such Reconsideration two thirds of that House shall agree to pass the Bill, it shall be sent, together with the Objections, to the other House, by which it shall likewise be reconsidered, and if approved by two thirds of that House, it shall become a Law. But in all such Cases the Votes of both Houses shall be determined by yeas and Nays, and the Names of the Persons voting for and against the Bill shall be entered on the Journal of each House respectively. If any Bill shall not be returned by the President within ten Days (Sundays excepted) after it shall have been presented to him, the Same shall be a Law, in like Manner as if he had signed it, unless the

Congress by their Adjournment prevent its Return, in which Case it shall not be a Law.

Every Order, Resolution, or Vote to which the Concurrence of the Senate and House of Representatives may be necessary (except on a question of Adjournment) shall be presented to the President of the United States; and before the Same shall take Effect, shall be approved by him, or being disapproved by him, shall be repassed by two thirds of the Senate and House of Representatives, according to the Rules and Limitations prescribed in the Case of a Bill.

Section. 8. The Congress shall have Power To lay and collect Taxes, Duties, Imposts and Excises, to pay the Debts and provide for the common Defence and general Welfare of the United States; but all Duties, Imposts and Excises shall be uniform throughout the United States;

To borrow Money on the credit of the United States;

To regulate Commerce with foreign Nations, and among the several States, and with the Indian Tribes;

To establish an uniform Rule of Naturalization, and uniform Laws on the subject of Bankruptcies throughout the United States;

To coin Money, regulate the Value thereof, and of foreign Coin, and fix the Standard of Weights and Measures;

To provide for the Punishment of counterfeiting the Securities and current Coin of the United States;

To establish Post Offices and post Roads;

To promote the Progress of Science and useful Arts, by securing for limited Times to Authors and Inventors the exclusive Right to their respective Writings and Discoveries;

To constitute Tribunals inferior to the supreme Court;

To define and punish Piracies and Felonies committed on the high Seas, and Offences against the Law of Nations;

To declare War, grant Letters of Marque and Reprisal, and make Rules concerning Captures on Land and Water;

To raise and support Armies, but no Appropriation of Money to that Use shall be for a longer Term than two Years;

To provide and maintain a Navy;

To make Rules for the Government and Regulation of the land and naval Forces;

To provide for calling forth the Militia to execute the Laws of the Union, suppress Insurrections and repel Invasions;

To provide for organizing, arming, and disciplining, the Militia, and for governing such Part of them as may be employed in the Service of the United States, reserving to the States respectively, the Appointment of the Officers, and the Authority of training the Militia according to the discipline prescribed by Congress;

To exercise exclusive Legislation in all Cases whatsoever, over such District (not exceeding ten Miles square) as may, by Cession of particular States, and the Acceptance of Congress, become the Seat of the Government of the United States, and to exercise like Authority over all Places purchased by the Consent of the Legislature of the State in which the Same shall be, for the Erection of Forts, Magazines, Arsenals, dock-Yards, and other needful Buildings; —And

To make all Laws which shall be necessary and proper for carrying into Execution the foregoing Powers, and all other Powers vested by this Constitution in the

Government of the United States, or in any Department or Officer thereof.

Section. 9. The Migration or Importation of such Persons as any of the States now existing shall think proper to admit, shall not be prohibited by the Congress prior to the Year one thousand eight hundred and eight, but a Tax or duty may be imposed on such Importation, not exceeding ten dollars for each Person.

The Privilege of the Writ of Habeas Corpus shall not be suspended, unless when in Cases of Rebellion or Invasion the public Safety may require it.

No Bill of Attainder or ex post facto Law shall be passed.

No Capitation, or other direct, Tax shall be laid, unless in Proportion to the Census or enumeration herein before directed to be taken.[116]

No Tax or Duty shall be laid on Articles exported from any State.

No Preference shall be given by any Regulation of Commerce or Revenue to the Ports of one State over those of another; nor shall Vessels bound to, or from, one State, be obliged to enter, clear, or pay Duties in another.

No Money shall be drawn from the Treasury, but in Consequence of Appropriations made by Law; and a regular Statement and Account of the Receipts and Expenditures of all public Money shall be published from time to time.

No Title of Nobility shall be granted by the United States: And no Person holding any Office of Profit or Trust under them, shall, without the Consent of the Congress, accept of any present, Emolument, Office, or

---

[116] *See* Amend. XVI.

Title, of any kind whatever, from any King, Prince, or foreign State.

Section. 10. No State shall enter into any Treaty, Alliance, or Confederation; grant Letters of Marque and Reprisal; coin Money; emit Bills of Credit; make any Thing but gold and silver Coin a Tender in Payment of Debts; pass any Bill of Attainder, ex post facto Law, or Law impairing the Obligation of Contracts, or grant any Title of Nobility.

No State shall, without the Consent of the Congress, lay any Imposts or Duties on Imports or Exports, except what may be absolutely necessary for executing it's inspection Laws: and the net Produce of all Duties and Imposts, laid by any State on Imports or Exports, shall be for the Use of the Treasury of the United States; and all such Laws shall be subject to the Revision and Controul of the Congress.

No State shall, without the Consent of Congress, lay any Duty of Tonnage, keep Troops, or Ships of War in time of Peace, enter into any Agreement or Compact with another State, or with a foreign Power, or engage in War, unless actually invaded, or in such imminent Danger as will not admit of delay.

Article. II.

Section. 1. The executive Power shall be vested in a President of the United States of America. He shall hold his Office during the Term of four Years, and, together with the Vice President, chosen for the same Term, be elected, as follows:

Each State shall appoint, in such Manner as the Legislature thereof may direct, a Number of Electors, equal to the whole Number of Senators and

Representatives to which the State may be entitled in the Congress: but no Senator or Representative, or Person holding an Office of Trust or Profit under the United States, shall be appointed an Elector.

The Electors shall meet in their respective States, and vote by Ballot for two Persons, of whom one at least shall not be an Inhabitant of the same State with themselves. And they shall make a List of all the Persons voted for, and of the Number of Votes for each; which List they shall sign and certify, and transmit sealed to the Seat of the Government of the United States, directed to the President of the Senate. The President of the Senate shall, in the Presence of the Senate and House of Representatives, open all the Certificates, and the Votes shall then be counted. The Person having the greatest Number of Votes shall be the President, if such Number be a Majority of the whole Number of Electors appointed; and if there be more than one who have such Majority, and have an equal Number of Votes, then the House of Representatives shall immediately chuse by Ballot one of them for President; and if no Person have a Majority, then from the five highest on the List the said House shall in like Manner chuse the President. But in chusing the President, the Votes shall be taken by States, the Representation from each State having one Vote; A quorum for this purpose shall consist of a Member or Members from two thirds of the States, and a Majority of all the States shall be necessary to a Choice. In every Case, after the Choice of the President, the Person having the greatest Number of Votes of the Electors shall be the Vice President. But if there should remain two or more who have equal Votes, the Senate shall chuse from them by Ballot the Vice President.[117]

The Congress may determine the Time of chusing the Electors, and the Day on which they shall give their Votes; which Day shall be the same throughout the United States.

No Person except a natural born Citizen, or a Citizen of the United States, at the time of the Adoption of this Constitution, shall be eligible to the Office of President; neither shall any Person be eligible to that Office who shall not have attained to the Age of thirty five Years, and been fourteen Years a Resident within the United States.

In Case of the Removal of the President from Office, or of his Death, Resignation, or Inability to discharge the Powers and Duties of the said Office, the Same shall devolve on the Vice President, and the Congress may by Law provide for the Case of Removal, Death, Resignation or Inability, both of the President and Vice President, declaring what Officer shall then act as President, and such Officer shall act accordingly, until the Disability be removed, or a President shall be elected.[118]

The President shall, at stated Times, receive for his Services, a Compensation, which shall neither be increased nor diminished during the Period for which he shall have been elected, and he shall not receive within that Period any other Emolument from the United States, or any of them.

---

[117] *See* Amend. XII.
[118] *See* Amend. XXV.

Before he enter on the Execution of his Office, he shall take the following Oath or Affirmation: —"I do solemnly swear (or affirm) that I will faithfully execute the Office of President of the United States, and will to the best of my Ability, preserve, protect and defend the Constitution of the United States."

Section. 2. The President shall be Commander in Chief of the Army and Navy of the United States, and of the Militia of the several States, when called into the actual Service of the United States; he may require the Opinion, in writing, of the principal Officer in each of the executive Departments, upon any Subject relating to the Duties of their respective Offices, and he shall have Power to grant Reprieves and Pardons for Offences against the United States, except in Cases of Impeachment.

He shall have Power, by and with the Advice and Consent of the Senate, to make Treaties, provided two thirds of the Senators present concur; and he shall nominate, and by and with the Advice and Consent of the Senate, shall appoint Ambassadors, other public Ministers and Consuls, Judges of the supreme Court, and all other Officers of the United States, whose Appointments are not herein otherwise provided for, and which shall be established by Law: but the Congress may by Law vest the Appointment of such inferior Officers, as they think proper, in the President alone, in the Courts of Law, or in the Heads of Departments.

The President shall have Power to fill up all Vacancies that may happen during the Recess of the Senate, by granting Commissions which shall expire at the End of their next Session.

Section. 3. He shall from time to time give to the Congress Information of the State of the Union, and recommend to their Consideration such Measures as he shall judge necessary and expedient; he may, on extraordinary Occasions, convene both Houses, or either of them, and in Case of Disagreement between them, with Respect to the Time of Adjournment, he may adjourn them to such Time as he shall think proper; he shall receive Ambassadors and other public Ministers; he shall take Care that the Laws be faithfully executed, and shall Commission all the Officers of the United States.

Section. 4. The President, Vice President and all civil Officers of the United States, shall be removed from Office on Impeachment for, and Conviction of, Treason, Bribery, or other high Crimes and Misdemeanors.

Article III.

Section. 1. The judicial Power of the United States shall be vested in one supreme Court, and in such inferior Courts as the Congress may from time to time ordain and establish. The Judges, both of the supreme and inferior Courts, shall hold their Offices during good Behaviour, and shall, at stated Times, receive for their Services a Compensation, which shall not be diminished during their Continuance in Office.

Section. 2. The judicial Power shall extend to all Cases, in Law and Equity, arising under this Constitution, the Laws of the United States, and Treaties made, or which shall be made, under their Authority; —to all Cases affecting Ambassadors, other public Ministers and Consuls; —to all Cases of admiralty and maritime Jurisdiction; —to Controversies to which the United States shall be a Party; —to Controversies between two or more States; —between a State and Citizens of another State,[119] —between Citizens of different States, —between Citizens of the same State claiming Lands under Grants of different States, and between a State, or the Citizens thereof, and foreign States, Citizens or Subjects.[120]

In all Cases affecting Ambassadors, other public Ministers and Consuls, and those in which a State shall be Party, the supreme Court shall have original Jurisdiction. In all the other Cases before mentioned, the supreme Court shall have appellate Jurisdiction, both as to Law and Fact, with such Exceptions, and under such Regulations as the Congress shall make.

The Trial of all Crimes, except in Cases of Impeachment, shall be by Jury; and such Trial shall be held in the State where the said Crimes shall have been committed; but when not committed within any State, the Trial shall be at such Place or Places as the Congress may by Law have directed.

Section. 3. Treason against the United States, shall consist only in levying War against them, or in adhering to their Enemies, giving them Aid and Comfort. No Person shall be convicted of Treason unless on the Testimony of two Witnesses to the same overt Act, or on Confession in open Court.

The Congress shall have Power to declare the Punishment of Treason, but no Attainder of Treason shall work Corruption of Blood, or Forfeiture except during the Life of the Person attainted.

---

[119] *See* Amend. XI.
[120] *See* Amend. XI.

Article. IV.

Section. 1. Full Faith and Credit shall be given in each State to the public Acts, Records, and judicial Proceedings of every other State. And the Congress may by general Laws prescribe the Manner in which such Acts, Records and Proceedings shall be proved, and the Effect thereof.

Section. 2. The Citizens of each State shall be entitled to all Privileges and Immunities of Citizens in the several States.

A Person charged in any State with Treason, Felony, or other Crime, who shall flee from Justice, and be found in another State, shall on Demand of the executive Authority of the State from which he fled, be delivered up, to be removed to the State having Jurisdiction of the Crime.

No Person held to Service or Labour in one State, under the Laws thereof, escaping into another, shall, in Consequence of any Law or Regulation therein, be discharged from such Service or Labour, but shall be delivered up on Claim of the Party to whom such Service or Labour may be due.[121]

Section. 3. New States may be admitted by the Congress into this Union; but no new State shall be formed or erected within the Jurisdiction of any other State; nor any State be formed by the Junction of two or more States, or Parts of States, without the Consent of the Legislatures of the States concerned as well as of the Congress.

The Congress shall have Power to dispose of and make all needful Rules and Regulations respecting the

---

[121] *See* Amend. XIII.

Territory or other Property belonging to the United States; and nothing in this Constitution shall be so construed as to Prejudice any Claims of the United States, or of any particular State.

Section. 4. The United States shall guarantee to every State in this Union a Republican Form of Government, and shall protect each of them against Invasion; and on Application of the Legislature, or of the Executive (when the Legislature cannot be convened), against domestic Violence.

Article. V.

The Congress, whenever two thirds of both Houses shall deem it necessary, shall propose Amendments to this Constitution, or, on the Application of the Legislatures of two thirds of the several States, shall call a Convention for proposing Amendments, which, in either Case, shall be valid to all Intents and Purposes, as Part of this Constitution, when ratified by the Legislatures of three fourths of the several States, or by Conventions in three fourths thereof, as the one or the other Mode of Ratification may be proposed by the Congress; Provided that no Amendment which may be made prior to the Year One thousand eight hundred and eight shall in any Manner affect the first and fourth Clauses in the Ninth Section of the first Article; and that no State, without its Consent, shall be deprived of its equal Suffrage in the Senate.

Article. VI.

All Debts contracted and Engagements entered into, before the Adoption of this Constitution, shall be as valid against the United States under this Constitution, as under the Confederation.

This Constitution, and the Laws of the United States which shall be made in Pursuance thereof; and all Treaties made, or which shall be made, under the Authority of the United States, shall be the supreme Law of the Land; and the Judges in every State shall be bound thereby, any Thing in the Constitution or Laws of any State to the Contrary notwithstanding.

The Senators and Representatives before mentioned, and the Members of the several State Legislatures, and all executive and judicial Officers, both of the United States and of the several States, shall be bound by Oath or Affirmation, to support this Constitution; but no religious Test shall ever be required as a Qualification to any Office or public Trust under the United States.

Article. VII.

The Ratification of the Conventions of nine States, shall be sufficient for the Establishment of this Constitution between the States so ratifying the Same.

The Word, "the," being interlined between the seventh and eighth Lines of the first Page, the Word "Thirty" being partly written on an Erazure in the fifteenth Line of the first Page, The Words "is tried" being interlined between the thirty second and thirty third Lines of the first Page and the Word "the" being interlined between the forty third and forty fourth Lines of the second Page.

Attest William Jackson Secretary

done in Convention by the Unanimous Consent of the States present the Seventeenth Day of September in the Year of our Lord one thousand seven hundred and Eighty seven and of the Independence of the United

States of America the Twelfth In witness whereof We
have hereunto subscribed our Names,

G°. Washington
Presidt and deputy from Virginia

Delaware
    Geo: Read
    Gunning Bedford jun
    John Dickinson
    Richard Bassett
    Jaco: Broom

Maryland
    James McHenry
    Dan of St Thos. Jenifer
    Danl. Carroll

Virginia
    John Blair
    James Madison Jr.

North Carolina
    Wm. Blount
    Richd. Dobbs Spaight
    Hu Williamson

South Carolina
    J. Rutledge
    Charles Cotesworth Pinckney
    Charles Pinckney
    Pierce Butler

Georgia
    William Few
    Abr Baldwin

New Hampshire
    John Langdon
    Nicholas Gilman

Massachusetts
    Nathaniel Gorham
    Rufus King

Connecticut
    Wm. Saml. Johnson
    Roger Sherman

New York
    Alexander Hamilton

New Jersey
    Wil: Livingston
    David Brearley
    Wm. Paterson
    Jona: Dayton

Pennsylvania
    B Franklin
    Thomas Mifflin
    Robt. Morris
    Geo. Clymer
    Thos. FitzSimons
    Jared Ingersoll
    James Wilson
    Gouv Morris

Congress of the United States,
begun and held at the City of New-York,
on Wednesday the fourth of March,
one thousand seven hundred and eighty nine.

THE Conventions of a number of the States, having at the time of their adopting the Constitution, expressed a desire, in order to prevent misconstruction or abuse of its powers, that further declaratory and restrictive clauses should be added: And as extending the ground of public confidence in the Government, will best ensure the beneficent ends of its institution.

RESOLVED by the Senate and House of Representatives of the United States of America, in Congress assembled, two thirds of both Houses concurring, that the following Articles be proposed to the Legislatures of the several States, as amendments to the Constitution of the United States, all, or any of which Articles, when ratified by three fourths of the said Legislatures, to be valid to all intents and purposes, as part of the said Constitution; viz.

ARTICLES in addition to, and Amendment of the Constitution of the United States of America, proposed by Congress, and ratified by the Legislatures of the several States, pursuant to the fifth Article of the original Constitution.

Amendment I.
Congress shall make no law respecting an establishment of religion, or prohibiting the free exercise thereof; or abridging the freedom of speech, or of the press; or the right of the people peaceably to assemble, and to petition the Government for a redress of grievances.

Amendment II.
A well regulated Militia, being necessary to the security of a free State, the right of the people to keep and bear Arms, shall not be infringed.

Amendment III.
No Soldier shall, in time of peace be quartered in any house, without the consent of the Owner, nor in time of war, but in a manner to be prescribed by law.

Amendment IV.
The right of the people to be secure in their persons, houses, papers, and effects, against unreasonable searches and seizures, shall not be violated, and no Warrants shall issue, but upon probable cause, supported by Oath or affirmation, and particularly describing the place to be searched, and the persons or things to be seized.

Amendment V.
No person shall be held to answer for a capital, or otherwise infamous crime, unless on a presentment or indictment of a Grand Jury, except in cases arising in the land or naval forces, or in the Militia, when in actual service in time of War or public danger; nor shall any person be subject for the same offence to be twice put in jeopardy of life or limb; nor shall be compelled in any criminal case to be a witness against himself, nor be deprived of life, liberty, or property, without due process of law; nor shall private property be taken for public use, without just compensation.

Amendment VI.

In all criminal prosecutions, the accused shall enjoy the right to a speedy and public trial, by an impartial jury of the State and district wherein the crime shall have been committed, which district shall have been previously ascertained by law, and to be informed of the nature and cause of the accusation; to be confronted with the witnesses against him; to have compulsory process for obtaining witnesses in his favor, and to have the Assistance of Counsel for his defence.

Amendment VII.

In Suits at common law, where the value in controversy shall exceed twenty dollars, the right of trial by jury shall be preserved, and no fact tried by a jury, shall be otherwise re-examined in any Court of the United States, than according to the rules of the common law.

Amendment VIII.

Excessive bail shall not be required, nor excessive fines imposed, nor cruel and unusual punishments inflicted.

Amendment IX.

The enumeration in the Constitution, of certain rights, shall not be construed to deny or disparage others retained by the people.

Amendment X.

The powers not delegated to the United States by the Constitution, nor prohibited by it to the States, are reserved to the States respectively, or to the people.

AMENDMENT XI

Passed by Congress March 4, 1794. Ratified February 7, 1795.

Note: Article III, section 2, of the Constitution was modified by amendment 11.

The Judicial power of the United States shall not be construed to extend to any suit in law or equity, commenced or prosecuted against one of the United States by Citizens of another State, or by Citizens or Subjects of any Foreign State.

AMENDMENT XII

Passed by Congress December 9, 1803. Ratified June 15, 1804.

Note: A portion of Article II, section 1 of the Constitution was superseded by the 12th amendment.

The Electors shall meet in their respective states and vote by ballot for President and Vice-President, one of whom, at least, shall not be an inhabitant of the same state with themselves; they shall name in their ballots the person voted for as President, and in distinct ballots the person voted for as Vice-President, and they shall make distinct lists of all persons voted for as President, and of all persons voted for as Vice-President, and of the number of votes for each, which lists they shall sign and certify, and transmit sealed to the seat of the government of the United States, directed to the President of the Senate; — the President of the Senate shall, in the presence of the Senate and House of Representatives, open all the certificates and the votes shall then be counted; —The person having the greatest number of votes for President, shall be the President, if such number be a majority of the whole number of Electors appointed; and if no person have such majority, then from the persons having the highest numbers not exceeding three on the list of those voted for as President, the House of Representatives shall choose immediately, by ballot, the President. But in choosing the President, the votes shall be taken by states, the representation from each state having one vote; a quorum for this purpose shall consist of a member or members from two-thirds of the states, and a majority of all the states shall be necessary to a choice. [And if the House of Representatives shall not choose a President whenever the right of choice shall devolve upon them, before the fourth day of March next following, then the Vice-President shall act as President, as in case of the death or other constitutional disability of the President.—]* The person having the greatest number of votes as Vice-President, shall be the Vice-President, if such number be a majority of the whole number of Electors appointed, and if no person have a majority, then from the two highest numbers on the list, the Senate shall choose the Vice-President; a quorum for the purpose shall consist of two-thirds of the whole number of Senators, and a majority of the whole number shall be necessary to a choice. But no person constitutionally ineligible to the office of President shall be eligible to that of Vice-President of the United States.

*Superseded by section 3 of the 20th amendment.

AMENDMENT XIII

Passed by Congress January 31, 1865. Ratified December 6, 1865.

Note: A portion of Article IV, section 2, of the Constitution was superseded by the 13th amendment.

Section 1. Neither slavery nor involuntary servitude, except as a punishment for crime whereof the party shall have been duly convicted, shall exist within the United States, or any place subject to their jurisdiction.

Section 2. Congress shall have power to enforce this article by appropriate legislation.

AMENDMENT XIV

Passed by Congress June 13, 1866. Ratified July 9, 1868. Note: Article I, section 2, of the Constitution was modified by section 2 of the 14th amendment.

Section 1. All persons born or naturalized in the United States, and subject to the jurisdiction thereof, are citizens of the United States and of the State wherein they reside. No State shall make or enforce any law which shall abridge the privileges or immunities of citizens of the United States; nor shall any State deprive any person of life, liberty, or property, without due process of law; nor deny to any person within its jurisdiction the equal protection of the laws.

Section 2. Representatives shall be apportioned among the several States according to their respective numbers, counting the whole number of persons in each State, excluding Indians not taxed. But when the right to vote at any election for the choice of electors for President and Vice-President of the United States, Representatives in Congress, the Executive and Judicial officers of a State, or the members of the Legislature thereof, is denied to any of the male inhabitants of such State, being twenty-one years of age,* and citizens of the United States, or in any way abridged, except for participation in rebellion, or other crime, the basis of representation therein shall be reduced in the proportion which the number of such male citizens shall bear to the whole number of male citizens twenty-one years of age in such State.

Section 3. No person shall be a Senator or Representative in Congress, or elector of President and Vice-President, or hold any office, civil or military, under the United States, or under any State, who, having previously taken an oath, as a member of Congress, or as an officer of the United States, or as a member of any State legislature, or as an executive or judicial officer of any State, to support the Constitution of the United States, shall have engaged in insurrection or rebellion against the same, or given aid or comfort to the enemies thereof. But Congress may by a vote of two-thirds of each House, remove such disability.

Section 4. The validity of the public debt of the United States, authorized by law, including debts incurred for payment of pensions and bounties for services in suppressing insurrection or rebellion, shall not be questioned. But neither the United States nor any State shall assume or pay any debt or obligation incurred in aid of insurrection or rebellion against the United States, or any claim for the loss or emancipation of any slave; but all such debts, obligations and claims shall be held illegal and void.

Section 5. The Congress shall have the power to enforce, by appropriate legislation, the provisions of this article.

*Changed by section 1 of the 26th amendment.

AMENDMENT XV

Passed by Congress February 26, 1869. Ratified February 3, 1870.

Section 1. The right of citizens of the United States to vote shall not be denied or abridged by the United States or by any State on account of race, color, or previous condition of servitude —

Section 2. The Congress shall have the power to enforce this article by appropriate legislation.

AMENDMENT XVI

Passed by Congress July 2, 1909. Ratified February 3, 1913.

Note: Article I, section 9, of the Constitution was modified by amendment 16.

The Congress shall have power to lay and collect taxes on incomes, from whatever source derived, without apportionment among the several States, and without regard to any census or enumeration.

AMENDMENT XVII

Passed by Congress May 13, 1912. Ratified April 8, 1913.

Note: Article I, section 3, of the Constitution was modified by the 17th amendment.

The Senate of the United States shall be composed of two Senators from each State, elected by the people thereof, for six years; and each Senator shall have one vote. The electors in each State shall have the qualifications requisite for electors of the most numerous branch of the State legislatures.

When vacancies happen in the representation of any State in the Senate, the executive authority of such State shall issue writs of election to fill such vacancies: *Provided,* That the legislature of any State may empower the executive thereof to make temporary appointments until the people fill the vacancies by election as the legislature may direct.

This amendment shall not be so construed as to affect the election or term of any Senator chosen before it becomes valid as part of the Constitution.

AMENDMENT XVIII

Passed by Congress December 18, 1917. Ratified January 16, 1919. Repealed by amendment 21.

Section 1. After one year from the ratification of this article the manufacture, sale, or transportation of intoxicating liquors within, the importation thereof into, or the exportation thereof from the United States and all territory subject to the jurisdiction thereof for beverage purposes is hereby prohibited.

Section 2. The Congress and the several States shall have concurrent power to enforce this article by appropriate legislation.

Section 3. This article shall be inoperative unless it shall have been ratified as an amendment to the Constitution by the legislatures of the several States, as provided in the Constitution, within seven years from the date of the submission hereof to the States by the Congress.

AMENDMENT XIX

Passed by Congress June 4, 1919. Ratified August 18, 1920.

The right of citizens of the United States to vote shall not be denied or abridged by the United States or by any State on account of sex.
Congress shall have power to enforce this article by appropriate legislation.

AMENDMENT XX

Passed by Congress March 2, 1932. Ratified January 23, 1933.

Note: Article I, section 4, of the Constitution was modified by section 2 of this amendment. In addition, a portion of the 12th amendment was superseded by section 3.

Section 1. The terms of the President and the Vice President shall end at noon on the 20th day of January, and the terms of Senators and Representatives at noon on the 3d day of January, of the years in which such terms would have ended if this article had not been ratified; and the terms of their successors shall then begin.

Section 2. The Congress shall assemble at least once in every year, and such meeting shall begin at noon on the 3d day of January, unless they shall by law appoint a different day.

Section 3. If, at the time fixed for the beginning of the term of the President, the President elect shall have died, the Vice President elect shall become President. If a President shall not have been chosen before the time fixed for the beginning of his term, or if the President elect shall have failed to qualify, then the Vice President elect shall act as President until a President shall have qualified; and the Congress may by law provide for the case wherein neither a President elect nor a Vice President shall have qualified, declaring who shall then act as President, or the manner in which one who is to act shall be selected, and such person shall act accordingly until a President or Vice President shall have qualified.

Section 4. The Congress may by law provide for the case of the death of any of the persons from whom the House of Representatives may choose a President whenever the right of choice shall have devolved upon them, and for the case of the death of any of the persons from whom the Senate may choose a Vice President whenever the right of choice shall have devolved upon them.

Section 5. Sections 1 and 2 shall take effect on the 15th day of October following the ratification of this article.

Section 6. This article shall be inoperative unless it shall have been ratified as an amendment to the Constitution by the legislatures of three-fourths of the several States within seven years from the date of its submission.

AMENDMENT XXI

Passed by Congress February 20, 1933. Ratified December 5, 1933.

Section 1. The eighteenth article of amendment to the Constitution of the United States is hereby repealed.

Section 2. The transportation or importation into any State, Territory, or Possession of the United States for delivery or use therein of intoxicating liquors, in violation of the laws thereof, is hereby prohibited.

Section 3. This article shall be inoperative unless it shall have been ratified as an amendment to the Constitution by conventions in the several States, as provided in the Constitution, within seven years from the date of the submission hereof to the States by the Congress.

AMENDMENT XXII

Passed by Congress March 21, 1947. Ratified February 27, 1951.

Section 1. No person shall be elected to the office of the President more than twice, and no person who has held the office of President, or acted as President, for more than two years of a term to which some other person was elected President shall be elected to the office of President more than once. But this Article shall not apply to any person holding the office of President when this Article was proposed by Congress, and shall not prevent any person who may be holding the office of President, or acting as President, during the term within which this Article becomes operative from holding the office of President or acting as President during the remainder of such term.

Section 2. This article shall be inoperative unless it shall have been ratified as an amendment to the Constitution by the legislatures of three-fourths of the several States within seven years from the date of its submission to the States by the Congress.

AMENDMENT XXIII

Passed by Congress June 16, 1960. Ratified March 29, 1961.

Section 1. The District constituting the seat of Government of the United States shall appoint in such manner as Congress may direct:

A number of electors of President and Vice President equal to the whole number of Senators and Representatives in Congress to which the District would be entitled if it were a State, but in no event more than the least populous State; they shall be in addition to those appointed by the States, but they shall be considered, for the purposes of the election of President and Vice President, to be electors appointed by a State; and they shall meet in the District and perform such duties as provided by the twelfth article of amendment.

Section 2. The Congress shall have power to enforce this article by appropriate legislation.

AMENDMENT XXIV

Passed by Congress August 27, 1962. Ratified January 23, 1964.

Section 1. The right of citizens of the United States to vote in any primary or other election for President or Vice President, for electors for President or Vice President, or for Senator or Representative in Congress, shall not be denied or abridged by the United States or any State by reason of failure to pay any poll tax or other tax.

Section 2. The Congress shall have power to enforce this article by appropriate legislation.

AMENDMENT XXV

Passed by Congress July 6, 1965. Ratified February 10, 1967.

Note: Article II, section 1, of the Constitution was affected by the 25th amendment.

Section 1. In case of the removal of the President from office or of his death or resignation, the Vice President shall become President.

Section 2. Whenever there is a vacancy in the office of the Vice President, the President shall nominate a Vice President who shall take office upon confirmation by a majority vote of both Houses of Congress.

Section 3. Whenever the President transmits to the President pro tempore of the Senate and the Speaker of the House of Representatives his written declaration that he is unable to discharge the powers and duties of his office, and until he transmits to them a written declaration to the contrary, such powers and duties shall be discharged by the Vice President as Acting President.

Section 4. Whenever the Vice President and a majority of either the principal officers of the executive departments or of such other body as Congress may by law provide, transmit to the President pro tempore of the Senate and the Speaker of the House of Representatives their written declaration that the President is unable to discharge the powers and duties of his office, the Vice President shall immediately assume the powers and duties of the office as Acting President.

Thereafter, when the President transmits to the President pro tempore of the Senate and the Speaker of the House of Representatives his written declaration that no inability exists, he shall resume the powers and duties of his office unless the Vice President and a majority of either the principal officers of the executive department or of such other body as Congress may by law provide, transmit within four days to the President pro tempore of the Senate and the Speaker of the House of Representatives their written declaration that the President is unable to discharge the powers and duties of his office. Thereupon Congress shall decide the issue, assembling within forty-eight hours for that purpose if not in session. If the Congress, within twenty-one days after receipt of the latter written declaration, or, if Congress is not in session, within twenty-one days after Congress is required to assemble, determines by two-thirds vote of both Houses that the President is unable to discharge the powers and duties of his office, the Vice President shall continue to discharge the same as Acting President; otherwise, the President shall resume the powers and duties of his office.

AMENDMENT XXVI

Passed by Congress March 23, 1971. Ratified July 1, 1971.

Note: Amendment 14, section 2, of the Constitution was modified by section 1 of the 26th amendment.

Section 1. The right of citizens of the United States, who are eighteen years of age or older, to vote shall not be denied or abridged by the United States or by any State on account of age.

Section 2. The Congress shall have power to enforce this article by appropriate legislation.

AMENDMENT XXVII
Originally proposed Sept. 25, 1789. Ratified May 7, 1992.

No law, varying the compensation for the services of the Senators and Representatives, shall take effect, until an election of representatives shall have intervened.

United States *n pl, sing* **United States**
[fr. The *United States* of America]
usu cap **:** the collective name of the
several north American bodies politic
joined together governmentally
by and under a supreme constitution :
a : one of these United States :
(1) an independent State < *Kansas is*
a free State > (2) a state government
as a component unit of a federal system
b : the name of a sovereign analogous to
other sovereigns in the family of nations
c : the national government as a
component unit of a federal system : as
< *there are many definitions of the term*
~ *throughout federal law* >

HARVARD

LAW REVIEW.

| VOL. XII. | JANUARY 25, 1899. | No. 6 |

THE STATUS OF OUR NEW TERRITORIES.[1]

WHAT extent of territory do the United States of America comprise? In order to answer this question intelligently, it is necessary to ascertain the meaning of the term "United States."

First. — It is the collective name of the States which are united together by and under the Constitution of the United States; and, prior to the adoption of that Constitution, and subsequently to the Declaration of Independence, it was the collective name of the thirteen States which made that Declaration, and which, from the time of the adoption of the Articles of Confederation to that of the adoption of the Constitution, were united together by and under the former. This, moreover, is the original, natural, and literal meaning of the term. Between the time of the first meeting of the Continental Congress, and that of the Declaration of Independence, the term "United Colonies" came into general use,[2] and, upon in-

---

[1] The following article was already planned, and in part written, when the writer first learned of Mr. Randolph's intention to furnish an article on the same general subject for the January number of this Review. While, therefore, the writer desires to acknowledge the material assistance which he has derived from Mr. Randolph's article, he entirely disclaims any intention to answer it, or to criticise it.

[2] It first occurs in the Journal of the Continental Congress, under date of June 7, 1775, vol. I. (ed. of 1777), p. 114 ["Resolved, that Thursday, the 20th of July next, be observed throughout the twelve United Colonies, as a day of humiliation, fasting, and prayer"]; and, from that time to the date of the Declaration of Independence, its use is very frequent. It occurs three times in the commission issued to Washington as commander-in-chief (p. 122), six times in the articles of war (pp. 133, 137, 138, 139, 140), and twice in the Declaration of the United Colonies of North America, under date of July 6, 1775, setting forth the causes and necessity of their taking up arms

dependence being declared, as the thirteen colonies became the thirteen States, the term was of course changed to "United States." In the Declaration of Independence both terms are used.[1] When the Articles of Confederation were framed, "United States of America" was declared to be the name and style of the confederation created by those articles.[2] This, however, had no other effect than to confirm the existing practice, and to increase the use of the term in the sense which it had already acquired; and accordingly, during the whole period of the Confederation, "United States" meant the same as "the thirteen United States," and the primary reason for using either term was to save the necessity of enumerating the thirteen States by name.

Indeed, the Articles of Confederation were merely an agreement between the thirteen States in their corporate capacity, or, more correctly, an agreement by each of the thirteen States with all the others. There were, therefore, thirteen parties to the confederation, and no more, and the people of the different States as individuals had directly no relations with it. Accordingly, it was the States in their corporate capacity that voted in the Continental Congress, and not the individual members of the Congress; and hence the voting power of a State did not at all depend upon the number of its delegates in Congress, and in fact each State was left to determine for itself, within certain limits, how many delegates it would send.[3] Hence also each State had the same voting power.[4] Even the style of the Continental Congress was "The United States in

---

(pp. 143, 145). Sometimes the number of United Colonies was specified, and sometimes it was not. The colony of Georgia did not unite with the other twelve, and so was not represented by delegates in Congress, until the thirteenth of September, 1775 (p. 197). Prior to that date, therefore, the term used was either the United Colonies, or the twelve United Colonies, while after that date it was either the United Colonies, or the thirteen United Colonies.

While this term was making its way to the front, it had a competitor (which was even earlier in the field), in the term "Continent" or "Continental," which was also much used during the war of the Revolution. Perhaps an attentive study of the Journal of Congress would show that "Continent" or "Continental" was not precisely synonymous with United Colonies or United States, but it certainly was very nearly so.

[1] "United Colonies" is used once, namely, in the concluding paragraph, and "United States" is used twice, namely, in the title and in the concluding paragraph.

[2] Art. 1.

[3] By the fifth article of Confederation, no State was to be represented by less than two delegates, nor by more than seven.

[4] Namely, each State had one vote. (Fifth Article of Confederation.)

Congress assembled," — not (as the present style would suggest) "The Delegates of the United States in Congress assembled"; and if the style had been "The Thirteen United States in Congress assembled," the meaning would have been precisely the same.

Evidence to the same effect, as to the sense in which the term "United States" was used prior to the time of the adoption of the Constitution, is furnished by the treaties made during the period of the Confederation. Thus, the Treaty of Alliance made with France, February 6, 1778, begins:[1] "The Most Christian King and the United States of North America, namely, New Hampshire," etc. (enumerating the thirteen States). So the Treaty of Amity and Commerce, made with France the same day, begins:[2] "The Most Christian King and the thirteen United States of North America, New Hampshire," etc. So the Treaty of Amity and Commerce made with Holland, October 8, 1782, begins:[3] "Their High Mightinesses, the States-General of the United Netherlands, and the United States of America, namely, New Hampshire," etc. So the Treaty of Amity and Commerce made with Sweden, April 3, 1783, begins:[4] "The King of Sweden and the thirteen United States of North America, namely, New Hampshire," etc. Lastly, the Definitive Treaty of Peace with England, September 3, 1783, by which our independence was established, after a recital, proceeds thus:[5] "Art. 1. His Britannic Majesty acknowledges the said United States, namely, New Hampshire, &c., to be free, sovereign, and independent States; that he treats with them as such; and relinquishes all claims to the government, propriety, and territorial rights."

With the adoption of the Constitution there came a great change; for the Constitution was not an agreement, but a law, — a law, too, superior to all other laws, coming as it did from the ultimate source of all laws, namely, the people, and being expressly declared by them to be the supreme law of the land.[6] At the same time, however, it neither destroyed nor consolidated the States, nor even affected their integrity; and, though it was established by the people of the United States; yet it was not established by them as one people, nor was its establishment a single act; but, on the contrary, its establishment in each State was the act of

---

[1] 8 U. S. Stats. 6.	[2] Page 12.
[3] Page 32.	[4] Page 60.
[5] Page 80.	[6] Art. 6, sect. 2.

the people of that State; and if the people of any State had finally refused to ratify and adopt it, the consequence would have been that that State would have ceased to be one of the United States. Indeed, the Constitution and the Articles of Confederation differ from each other, in respect to the source of their authority, in one particular only, namely, that, while the former proceeded from the people of each State, the latter proceeded from the Legislature of each State. In respect to their effect and operation also, the two instruments differ from each other in one particular only, namely, that, while the Articles of Confederation merely imposed an obligation upon each State, in its corporate and sovereign capacity, in favor of the twelve other States, the Constitution binds as a law, not each *State*, but all persons and property in each State. These differences, moreover, fundamental and important as they undoubtedly are, do not, nor does either of them, at all affect either the meaning or the use of the term "United States"; and, therefore, the conclusion is that the meaning which that term had the day after Independence was declared, it still retains, and that this is its natural and literal meaning.

Regarded, then, as simply the collective name of all the States, do the United States comprise territory? Directly, they certainly do not; indirectly, they do comprise the territory of the forty-five States, and no more. That they comprise this territory only indirectly, appears from the fact that such territory will always be identical with the territory of all the States in the aggregate, — will increase as that increases, and diminish as that diminishes.

Secondly. — Since the adoption of the Constitution, the term "United States" has been the name of a sovereign, and that sovereign occupies a position analogous to that of the personal sovereigns of most European countries. Indeed, the analogy between them is closer, at least in one respect, than at first sight appears; for a natural person who is also a sovereign has two personalities, one natural, the other artificial and legal, and it is the latter that is sovereign. It is as true, therefore, of England (for example) as it is of this country, that her sovereign is an artificial and legal person (*i. e.*, a body politic and corporate), and, therefore, never dies. The difference between the two sovereigns is, that, while the former consists of a single person, the latter consists of many persons, each of whom is a member of the body politic. In short, while the former is a corporation sole, the latter is a corporation aggregate.

Who, then, are those persons of whom the United States as a body politic consists, and who constitute its members? Clearly they must be either the States in their corporate capacity, *i. e.*, artificial and legal persons, or the citizens of all the States in the aggregate; and it is not difficult to see that they are the former. Indeed, the latter do not form a political unit for any purpose. The citizens of each State form the body politic of that State, and the States form the body politic of the United States. The latter, therefore, consisted at first of the original thirteen States, just as the Confederation did; but, as often as a new State was admitted, a new member was received into the body politic, — which, therefore, now consists of forty-five members. It will be seen, therefore, that, while the United States, in its second sense, signifies the body politic created by the Constitution, in its first sense it signifies the members of that body politic in the aggregate. A consequence is that, while in its first sense the term "United States" is always plural, in its second sense it is in strictness always singular.

The State of New York furnishes a good illustration of the two senses in which the term "United States" is used under the Constitution; for the style of that State, as a body politic, is "The People of the State of New York," and the members of that body politic are the citizens of the State. The term "people," therefore, in that State, means, first, all the citizens of the State in the aggregate (*i. e.*, the members of the body politic), and, secondly, the body politic itself; and while in the former sense it is plural, in the latter sense it is singular.

The term "United States" is used in its second sense whenever it is used for the purpose of expressing legal or political relations between the United States and the particular States, or between the former and foreign sovereigns or states, or legal relations between the former and private persons, while it is used in its first and original sense whenever it is desired to designate the particular States collectively, either as such or as members of the body politic of the United States. It is also used in that sense whenever it is used to designate the territory of all the States in the aggregate.

As a substitute for the term "United States," when used in its second sense, the term "Union" is often employed. The original difference between "United States" and "Union" was that, while the former was concrete, the latter was abstract; and hence it is that the latter cannot be substituted for the former when used in its original sense.[1]

When used in its second sense, it is plain that the term "United States" has no reference to extent of territory, either directly or indirectly. Regarded as a body politic, the United States may and does own territory, and may be and is a sovereign over territory, but to speak of its constituting or comprising territory would be no less absurd than to predicate the same thing of a personal sovereign, though the absurdity would be less obvious.

Thirdly. — Since the treaty with England of September 3, 1783, the term "United States" has often been used to designate all territory over which the sovereignty of the United States extended. The occasion for so using the term could not of course arise until the United States acquired the sovereignty over territory outside the limits of any State, and they first acquired such territory by the treaty just referred to. For, although, as has been said, that treaty was made with each of the thirteen States, yet, in fixing the boundaries, the thirteen States were treated as constituting one country, England not being interested in the question how that country should be divided among the several States. Moreover, the boundaries established by the treaty embraced a considerable amount of territory in the Northwest to which no State had any separate claim, and which, therefore, belonged to the United States; and the territory thus acquired was enlarged from time to time by cessions from different States, until at length it embraced the entire region within the limits of the treaty, and west of Pennsylvania, Virginia, North Carolina, and Georgia, as the western boundaries of those States were afterwards established, with the exception of the territory now constituting the State of Kentucky. Then followed in succession the acquisitions from France, Spain, Texas, and Mexico. Out of all the territory thus acquired, twenty-eight great States have been from time to time carved; and yet there has never been a time, since the date of the treaty before referred to, when the United States had not a considerable amount of territory outside the limits of any State.

---

[1] The term "Union" is used three times in the Constitution, namely, in Art. 1, sect. 8, subsect. 15 [Congress shall have power "to provide for calling forth the militia to execute the laws of the Union, suppress insurrections, and repel invasions"]; in Art. 2, sect. 3 [the President "shall from time to time give to the Congress information of the state of the Union," &c.]; and in Art. 4, sect. 3, subsect. 1 ["new States may be admitted by the Congress into this Union"].

It is plain, therefore, that for one hundred and fifteen years there has been more or less need of some word or term by which to designate as well the Territories of the United States as the States themselves; and such word or term ought, moreover, to have been one signifying directly not territory, but sovereignty, sovereignty being the only thing that can be predicated alike of States and Territories. The same need was long since felt by England as well as by other European countries, and the word "empire" was adopted to satisfy it; and perhaps we should have adopted the same word, if we had felt the need of a new word or term more strongly. Two peculiarities have, however, hitherto characterized the territory held by the United States outside the limits of any State: first, such territory has been virtually a wilderness; secondly, it has been looked upon merely as material out of which new States were to be carved just as soon as there was sufficient population to warrant the taking of such a step; and hence the need of a single term which would embrace territories as well as States has not been greatly felt. At all events, no such new term has been adopted; and hence "United States" is the only term we have had to designate collectively either the States alone, or the States and Territories; and accordingly, while it has always been used for the former of these two purposes, it has also frequently been used for the latter.

It is very important, however, to understand that the use of the term "United States" to designate all territory over which the United States is sovereign, is, like the similar use of the word "empire" in England and other European countries, purely conventional; and that it has, therefore, no legal or constitutional significance. Indeed, this use of the term has no connection whatever with the Constitution of the United States, and the occasion for it would have been precisely the same if the Articles of Confederation had remained in force to the present day, assuming that, in other respects, our history had been what it has been.

The conclusion, therefore, is that, while the term "United States" has three meanings, only the first and second of these are known to the Constitution; and that is equivalent to saying that the Constitution of the United States as such does not extend beyond the limits of the States which are united by and under it, — a proposition the truth of which will, it is believed, be placed beyond doubt by an examination of the instances in which the term "United States" is used in the Constitution.

Its use first occurs in the preamble,[1] in which it is used twice.
The first time it is plainly used in its original sense, *i. e.*, as the collective name of the States which should adopt it. If the words had
been "We, the people of the thirteen[2] United States respectively," the sense in which "United States" was used would have
been precisely the same. Nor is there any doubt that it is used in
the same sense at the end of the preamble. Of course there is a
very strong presumption that when a constitution is made by a
sovereign people, it is made exclusively for the country inhabited
by that people, and exclusively for that people regarded as a body
politic, and so having perpetual succession; and the same thing
is true, *mutatis mutandis*, of a constitution made by the people of
several sovereign States united together for that purpose. The
preamble, however, does not leave it to presumption to determine
for what regions of country and what people the Constitution of
the United States was made; for it expressly declares that its
purposes and objects are, first, to form a more perfect union
(*i. e.*, among the thirteen States, or as many of them as shall
adopt it). Then follow four other objects which, though in terms
indefinite as to their territorial scope, are by clear implication
limited to the same States;[3] and lastly its purpose and object are

---

[1] "We the People of the United States, in order to form a more perfect Union, establish justice, insure domestic tranquillity, provide for the common defence, promote
the general welfare, and secure the blessings of Liberty to ourselves and our posterity,
do ordain and establish this Constitution for the United States of America."

[2] To have stated the number of States in the preamble would, however, have been
inconvenient, because it was uncertain, when the Constitution was framed, how many
States would adopt it. It was provided by Art. 7 that, as soon as it was adopted by
nine States, it should become binding upon the States adopting it, nine being within a
fraction of three-fourths of the whole, and the assent of nine States having been required
by the Articles of Confederation for the doing of all acts of prime importance. (See
Art. 9, last paragraph but one, and Arts. 10 and 11.) In fact, only eleven States partici-
pated in the first election of Washington as President, and only that number was represented in Congress during the first session of the first Congress.

[3] Moreover, the usage of the times furnishes positive proof that the terms "common defence" and "general welfare" were used in the preamble with exclusive reference to the thirteen States; for the words "common" and "general" were familiarly
used to distinguish what concerned the United States from what concerned the several
States as such, and that too at a time when "United States" could not possibly mean
anything else than the thirteen United States. Thus, the 3d Article of Confederation provides as follows: "The said States hereby severally enter into a firm league of
friendship with each other, for their 'common' defence, the security of their liberties,
and their mutual and 'general' welfare." So also the 5th Article contains the following: "For the more convenient management of the 'general' interest of the United
States, delegates shall be annually appointed . . . to meet in Congress." So also in

---

declared to be to secure the blessings of liberty to the people by whom it is ordained and established, and their successors; for, though the word used is "posterity," it is clearly not used with literal accuracy, but in the sense of "successors." According to the preamble, therefore, the Constitution is limited to the thirteen States which were united under the Articles of Confederation; and it is by virtue of Art. 4, sect. 3, subsect. 1,[1] and in spite of the preamble, that new States have been admitted upon an equal footing with the original thirteen.

In the phrases, "Congress of the United States,"[2] "Senate of the United States,"[3] "President of the United States," or "Vice President of the United States,"[4] "office under the United States,"[5] "officers of the United States,"[6] "on the credit of the United States,"[7] "securities and current coins of the United States,"[8] "service of the United States,"[9] "government of the United States,"[10] "granted by the United States,"[11] "Treasury of the United States,"[12] "Constitution of the United States,"[13] "army and navy of the United States,"[14] "offences against the United States,"[15] "judicial power of the United States,"[16] "laws of the United States,"[17] "controversies to which the United States shall be a party,"[18] "treason against the United States,"[19] "territory or other property belonging to the

the 7th Article are the words: "When land forces are raised by any State for the 'common' defence," etc. So in the 8th Article are the words: "All charges of war, and all other expenses that shall be incurred for the 'common' defence or 'general' welfare, and allowed by the United States in Congress assembled, shall be defrayed out of a 'common' treasury." Lastly, the 9th Article contains the following: "The United States in Congress assembled shall have authority to appoint such other committees and civil officers as may be necessary for managing the 'general' affairs of the United States under their direction."

[1] See *supra*, page 370, note 1.   [2] Art. 1, sect. 1; Art. 1, sect. 2, subsect. 3.

[3] Art. 1, sect. 3, subsect. 1.

[4] Art. 1, sect. 3, subsects. 4, 5, and 6; Art. 2, sect. 1, subsects. 1 and 8; 12th Amendment; 14th Amendment, sect. 2; Art. 1, sect. 7, subsects. 2 and 3.

[5] Art. 1, sect. 3, subsect. 7; Art. 1, sect. 9, subsect. 8; Art. 2, sect. 1, subsect. 2; Art. 6, subsect. 3; 14th Amendment, sect. 3; Art. 1, sect. 6, subsect. 2.

[6] Art. 2, sect. 2, subsect. 2, sect. 3, sect. 4; Art. 6, subsect. 3; 14th Amendment, sect. 3.

[7] Art. 1, sect. 8, subsect. 2.   [8] Art. 1, sect. 8, subsect. 6.

[9] Art. 1, sect. 8, subsect. 16; Art. 2, sect. 2, subsect. 1.

[10] Art. 1, sect. 8, subsects. 17 and 18; Art. 2, sect. 1, subsect. 3; 12th Amendment.

[11] Art. 1, sect. 9, subsect. 8.

[12] Art. 1, sect. 10, subsect. 2; Art. 1, sect. 6, subsect. 1.

[13] Art. 2, sect. 1, subsect. 8; 14th Amendment, sect. 3.

[14] Art. 2, sect. 2, subsect. 1.   [15] Art. 2, sect. 2, subsect. 1.

[16] Art. 3, sect. 1; 11th Amendment.

[17] Art. 3, sect. 2, subsect. 1; Art. 6, subsect. 2.

[18] Art. 3, sect. 2, subsect. 1.   [19] Art. 3, sect. 3, subsect. 1.

United States," [1] "claims of the United States," [2] "the United States shall guarantee," [3] "shall be valid against the United States," [4] "under the authority of the United States," [5] "court of the United States," [6] "delegated to the United States," [7] "public debt of the United States," [8] "insurrection or rebellion against the United States," [9] "shall not be denied or abridged by the United States," [10] "neither the United States nor any State shall assume or pay," [11] the term "United States" is used in its second sense.[12] It seems also to be used in the same sense in the phrase, "citizen of the United States;" [13] for it is only as a unit, a body politic, and a sovereign, that the United States can have citizens, — not as the collective name of forty-five States. In the phrase, "common

[1] Art. 4, sect. 3, subsect. 2.

[2] Art. 4, sect. 3, subsect. 2.

[3] Art. 3, sect. 4.

[4] Art. 6, subsect. 1.

[5] Art. 6, subsect. 2.

[6] 7th Amendment.

[7] 10th Amendment.

[8] 14th Amendment, sect. 4.

[9] 14th Amendment, sect. 4.

[10] 15th Amendment.

[11] 14th Amendment, sect. 4.

[12] As the second sense in which the term "United States" is used in the Constitution had no existence prior to the time of the adoption of the Constitution, it follows that, whenever the Articles of Confederation use the term in such phrases as any of those enumerated above or in similar phrases, they use it (as they do in all cases) in its original sense. Instances will be found in Art. 4 ["no imposition, duties, or restriction shall be laid by any State on the property of the United States or either of them"], Art. 5 ["nor shall any delegate hold any office under the United States," etc.], Art. 6 ["nor shall any person holding any office of profit or trust under the United States or any of them accept of any present," etc.], Art. 9 ["no State shall be deprived of territory for the benefit of the United States;" "nor ascertain the sums and expenditures necessary for the defence and welfare of the United States or any of them;" "in the service of the United States;" "Congress of the United States;" "on the credit of the United States;" "at the expense of the United States"], Art. 11 ["Canada acceding to this confederation, and joining in the measures of the United States, shall be admitted into, and entitled to all the advantages of, this Union"], Art. 12 ["shall be deemed and considered as a charge against the United States, for payment and satisfaction whereof the said United States and the public faith are hereby solemnly pledged"], and Art. 13 ["Congress of the United States"].

In most cases, however, in which the term "United States," in its second sense, or the term "Congress" or "Congress of the United States," would be used in the Constitution, the phrase "United States in Congress assembled" is used in the Articles of Confederation. That phrase occurs in those articles a great number of times, and, whenever it occurs, "United States" is used in its original sense. This is clearly brought out by the following words in Art. 5: "Each State shall maintain its own delegates in any meeting of the States;" also by the following words in Art. 10: "the voice of nine States in the Congress of the United States assembled;" and also by the following words in Art. 12: "before the assembling of the United States [not the delegates of the United States] in pursuance of the present confederation."

[13] Art. 1, sect. 2, subsect. 2; Art. 1, sect. 3, subsect. 3; Art. 2, sect. 1, subsect. 5; 14th Amendment, sects. 1 and 2; 15th Amendment, sect. 1.

defence and general welfare of the United States,"[1] it seems to be used in its first or original sense, especially as "common defence" and "general welfare" are taken from the preamble.[2] Certainly there is no pretence for saying it is used in its third sense. In the phrase, "throughout the United States,"[3] there is believed to be no doubt that it is used in its original sense,[4] though it may be claimed that it is used in its third sense.[5] That it is used in its original sense in one instance is certain;[6] and when the same phrase is used in different parts of the Constitution, a strong presumption arises that it is always used in the same sense.

In the phrase, "resident within the United States,"[7] there can be no doubt that "United States" is used in its original sense, the meaning being the same as if the words had been, "resident in one or more of the United States."

The phrase, "one of the United States," affords a good instance of the use of "United States" in its original sense.[8]

In the phrase, "shall not receive any other emolument from the United States or any of them,"[9] it is certain that "United States" is used in its second sense, though it is also certain that the draughtsman supposed he was using it in its original sense.[10]

---

[1] Art. 1, sect. 8, subsect. 1.   [2] See *supra*, page 372, and notes 1 and 3.

[3] Art. 1, sect. 8, subsects. 1 and 4; Art. 2, sect. 1, subsect. 3.

[4] It has been seen (*supra*, p. 365, n. 2) that the first time the term "United Colonies" occurs in the Journal of Congress, it is in the phrase, "throughout the twelve United Colonies." The phrase, "throughout the United States" is also used in two instances in the 9th Article of Confederation ["the United States in Congress assembled shall have the sole and exclusive right and power of fixing the standard of weights and measures throughout the United States . . . establishing or regulating Post Offices *from one State to another* throughout all the United States"], in neither of which can it possibly have any other meaning than throughout the thirteen United States. Can any reason then be given for supposing that the authors of the Constitution attached a wholly different meaning to the same phrase, namely, "throughout all the territory within the sovereignty of the United States"? It is believed that there cannot; and yet the question depends entirely upon intention. For the reader should bear in mind the fact that, while the term "United States" may have its second meaning in the Constitution, though it was previously used in the same phrase with its original meaning (and that, too, without any change of intention), it cannot, in the Constitution or elsewhere, have its third meaning, in a phrase in which it had previously had its first meaning, without a corresponding change of intention.

[5] See *infra*, page 381.

[6] Art. 2, sect. 1, subsect. 4 ["The Congress may determine the time of choosing the electors, and the day on which they shall give their votes; which day shall be the same throughout the United States"].   [7] Art. 2, sect. 1, subsect. 5.

[8] Art. 2, sect. 1, subsect. 7.   [9] 11th Amendment.

[10] At page 374, note 12, will be found an extract from the 4th Article of Confedera-

In the phrase, "all persons born or naturalized in the United States," [1] it seems clear that "United States" is used in its original sense; for, first, it is either used in that sense or in its third sense, and, as the latter is not a constitutional or legal sense, there is a presumption that the term is not used in that sense in an amendment of the Constitution; secondly, it is declared that the same persons shall be citizens of the State in which they reside, and this shows that the authors of the amendment contemplated only States, for, if they had contemplated Territories as well, they certainly would have said "citizens of the State or Territory in which they reside"; thirdly, the whole of the 14th Amendment had reference exclusively to the then late war, and was designed to secure its results, — in particular to secure to persons of African descent certain political rights, and to take from the States respectively in which they might reside the power to deprive them of those rights. Moreover, the amendment consists mainly of prohibitions, and these are all (with a single exception which need not be mentioned) aimed exclusively against the States. It was no part of the object of the amendment to restrain the power of Congress (which its authors did not distrust), and hence there was no practical reason for extending its operation to Territories, in which all the power resided in Congress. What is the true meaning of "United States" in the phrase under consideration is certainly a question of great moment, for on its answer depends the question whether all persons hereafter born in any of our recently acquired islands will be by birth citizens of the United States.

The foregoing comprise all the instances but one in which the term "United States" is used either in the original Constitution,

---

tion, in which occurs the phrase, "the United States or either of them," and also an extract from the 6th Article, in which occurs the phrase, "the United States or any of them;" and, while these phrases are perfectly correct where they stand, yet a transfer to the Constitution of the passages containing them would have made the same phrases incorrect, as such transfer would have changed the meaning of "United States." On the other hand, a transfer to the Constitution of an extract in the same note from Art. 9, containing the same phrase, would, it seems, have caused no change in the meaning of "United States," and hence the phrase in question would have been correct, notwithstanding such transfer.

[1] 14th Amendment, sect. 1: ["All persons born or naturalized in the United States, and subject to the jurisdiction thereof, are citizens of the United States and of the State wherein they reside. No State shall make or enforce any law which shall abridge the privileges or immunities of citizens of the United States; nor shall any State deprive any person of life, liberty, or property without due process of law; nor deny to any person within its jurisdiction the equal protection of the laws."]

or in any of its amendments. The other instance is found in the 13th Amendment,[1] — in which "United States" is plainly used in its original sense, if the words which follow it are to have any meaning; and yet, if the authors of that amendment had understood that the term "United States," when used in the Constitution to express extent of territory, had its third meaning, they would have omitted the words, "or any place subject to their jurisdiction."

If a broader view be taken of the Constitution and its amendments, it will be found that the only portions of it which indicate the slightest intention to extend their operation beyond the limits of the States, are the clause authorizing the admission of new States,[2] the clause providing for the government of territories,[3] and the 13th Amendment.

The Constitution of the United States, like other constitutions, is mainly occupied with the creation and organization of the three great departments of government, — the legislative, the executive, and the judicial. Accordingly, the first three articles, comprising about six-sevenths of the whole, are entirely occupied with these three departments respectively. The last three sections of Art. 1 (namely, the 8th, 9th, and 10th Sections) are, however, peculiar to the Constitution of the United States as a federal constitution, and will, therefore, be excluded from view for the present. Of the remainder of Art. 1, and of the whole of Arts. 2 and 3, it may be affirmed that not one word in either has any reference or any application to any territory outside the limits of the States. As to Arts. 1 and 2, the correctness of this view has never been questioned, and, as to Art. 3, its correctness is established by the uniform practice of the legislative department[4] of the govern-

---

[1] ["Neither slavery nor involuntary servitude, except as a punishment for crime, whereof the party shall have been duly convicted, shall exist within the United States or any place subject to their jurisdiction."]

[2] See *supra*, page 370, note 1.

[3] Art. 4, sect. 3, subsect. 2.

[4] For example, the entire judicial power in the Territories has always been vested by Congress in one set of courts, regardless of the dual system which exists in all the States by virtue of Art. 3 of the Constitution. Moreover, these courts have always been termed Territorial courts (not United States courts), and have always been so regarded; the statutes by which they have been created and governed are wholly separate and distinct from those creating and governing the courts of the United States within the States; their judges have generally held office only for a term of four years, whereas all judges appointed under Art. 3 of the Constitution hold office during good behavior; and originally there was no appeal from any Territorial court to the Supreme Court.

ment, and by a uniform course of decisions in the judicial department.[1]

A distinction must, however, be made between those articles of the Constitution by which the several departments of the government were respectively created and organized, and those departments themselves; for the reasoning which is applicable to the former is not necessarily applicable to the latter, nor is the same reasoning necessarily applicable to all of the latter. It does not follow, because a department of the government is created and organized by the Constitution with reference solely to a given territory, that, therefore, the power of that department and its sphere of action are limited to that territory. It may or may not be true, and it may be true of one department, and not true of another department. In fact, it is true of the judicial department, but it is not true of either the legislative or the executive department. How is it, then, that one of these three departments can differ so materially from the other two, when no such difference is indicated by the Constitution, which created and organized them all? It is because the difference depends, not upon the Constitution, but upon the nature of the departments themselves. The legislative and executive departments are sovereign in their nature, and, therefore, their power and sphere of action are co-extensive with the sovereignty of the United States, of which sovereignty they constitute the vital part, — of which, in fact, they constitute all that has been delegated. It is by them alone that the sovereignty of the United States can, without changing or overthrowing the present Constitution, either speak or act, *i. e.*, either declare its will, or execute that will when declared. The judicial department, on the other hand, is not the depositary of any portion of the sovereign power; its function is simply to judge; it cannot even enforce its own judgments; without the support of both the legislative and executive departments it could have no existence, other than theoretical, since the latter alone can appoint judges, and the former alone can provide them with salaries. It is true that the judicial department sometimes disregards what the legislative department has declared to be the sovereign will; but that is not because of the nature of the judicial office, — it is rather in spite

---

[1] Seré *v.* Pitot, 6 Cr. 332; Am. Ins. Co. *v.* Canter, 1 Pet. 511; Benner *v.* Porter, 9 How. 235; Clinton *v.* Englebrecht, 13 Wall. 434; Reynolds *v.* U. S., 98 U. S. 145; The City of Panama, 101 U. S. 453; McAllister *v.* U. S., 141 U. S. 174.

of it; it is not because it is the function of the judicial department to sit in judgment upon the action of the legislative department, but because the judicial department has held that it cannot
do otherwise than disregard an act of the legislative department
which is in violation of the Constitution, without itself. incurring
the guilt of violating the Constitution, and also (it may be added)
because the legislative department and the people have acquiesced
in that view.

While, therefore, the power of the legislative and executive departments is co-extensive with the sovereignty, the judicial department can exercise only such jurisdiction as has been delegated to
it; and hence its jurisdiction would still be limited to the original
thirteen States, had not the Constitution provided for the admission
of new States.

There is, therefore, no room for any question as to where either
the legislative, the executive, or the judicial power in our new territories resides; for the legislative power clearly resides in the
Congress of the United States, and the executive power in the
President of the United States; and the power of establishing
the judicial department also resides in Congress, though Congress
cannot itself exercise the power belonging to that department. In
the legislative and executive departments, therefore, is vested all
the sovereign power in our new territories that has been delegated
by the people; and the real question is in what character, and subject to what limitations, if any, do they hold this power. Does Congress (for example) hold the legislative power there as it does in the
States, *i. e.,* subject to all the limitations and restrictions imposed
by the Constitution; or does it hold that power in the new territories without any other limitation than that imposed by the
13th Amendment, namely, that it shall not establish slavery in
any of them; or does the truth lie somewhere between these two
extremes? And this brings us to the question whether the limitations and restrictions imposed upon Congress by the Constitution
are operative outside the States. These limitations and restrictions
are found chiefly in the 8th and 9th sections of Art. 1, and in the
first ten Amendments.

The 8th Section of Art. 1 owes its existence entirely to the fact
that the Constitution of the United States, while it is a true constitution, and creates a true sovereign, is yet a federal constitution.
By it the people of each State vested a portion of the sovereignty

of that State in the new sovereign created by the Constitution, *i. e.*, they made a partition of the sovereignty of the State between the State and the United States, and the 8th section of Art. 1 contains that partition. The mode of making it was by granting to the new sovereign those branches of sovereignty which are enumerated in the respective subsections of Section 8. That section, therefore, so far as regards its main object and scope, can have no application to any territory beyond the limits of the several States, for no partition was to be made of the sovereignty over any such territory. A strong presumption, therefore, arises that no part of the section was intended to extend beyond the limits of the States, as it cannot be supposed that any incidental objects were intended to have a more extensive operation than the main object.

What were the incidental objects of the section? One was to provide security that the United States, in exercising those branches of sovereignty which had been granted to it, should treat all the States alike; for, if no such security were provided, a majority of States might at any time combine to oppress a minority. Accordingly, subsection 1 having granted to Congress the power "to lay and collect taxes, duties, imposts, and excises," it is added "but all duties, imposts, and excises shall be uniform throughout the United States." So, also, subsection 4 grants to Congress the power to establish an "uniform" rule of naturalization, and "uniform" laws on the subject of bankruptcies "throughout the United States." Reasons have already been given for believing that the term "United States," in both these subsections, is used in its original sense; and we now find another argument, in favor of the same view, in the scope and object of Section 8. As it would be absurd to hold that the grant of power in these subsections had any reference to territories as distinguished from States, since Congress has full legislative powers in the territories without any grant from the States, so it would be absurd to hold that the limitation of the power has a more extensive operation than the power itself. Moreover, if all other arguments fail, it is at least true that those subsections contain nothing whatever to overthrow the presumption in favor of their being limited in their operation to the States.

There is a *dictum* by Chief Justice Marshall, in Loughborough v. Blake,[1] which is opposed to the view insisted upon in this article.

---

[1] 5 Wheat. 317.

It is, however, only a *dictum*, as the learned Chief Justice himself admits. The circumstances of the case were these. Jan. 9, 1815, Congress passed an Act [1] laying an annual direct tax of $6,000,000 upon the United States, which sum it proceeded to apportion among the eighteen then existing States. Feb. 27, 1815, Congress passed another Act,[2] which in effect extended the first Act to the District of Columbia. The plaintiff having refused to pay his share of the tax imposed upon the District by the second Act, claiming that the Act was unconstitutional, his property was seized, and he brought trespass against the officer making the seizure. The plaintiff's claim admitted of a very short answer, namely, that by Art. 1 of the Constitution, Section 8, subsection 17, Congress had all the power within the District that it had in any State *plus* the power of the legislature of that State, and, therefore, had an unqualified power of taxation. Still, the Chief Justice thought it desirable (for what reason is not very apparent) to show that Congress also had the power to impose the tax under the same grants of power by which it was authorized to pass the first Act. Accordingly, he said, first, the power given to Congress to lay and collect taxes was in terms without limitation as to place; secondly, the power to lay and collect taxes had the same extent as to place as the power to lay and collect duties, imposts, and excises; thirdly, the latter power was required to be exercised uniformly throughout the United States, and it could not be so exercised unless it extended throughout the United States; and this brought him to the question, what was meant by "United States" in the phrase, "throughout the United States." "Does this term," said he,[3] "designate the whole or any particular portion of the American Empire? Certainly this question can admit of but one answer. It is the name given to our great republic, which is composed of States and Territories. The District of Columbia, or the territory west of the Missouri, is not less within the United States than Maryland or Pennsylvania." If this *dictum* be taken as simply giving one of the meanings of the term "United States," and without reference to the Constitution, its correctness cannot be questioned; but it seems not to have occurred to its learned author that, while the meaning which he attributed to the term was one of its meanings, it had other meanings also;

---

[1] C. 21, 3 Stats. 164.   [2] C. 60, 3 Stats. 216.

[3] 5 Wheat. 319.

that it had been used in another sense in the first [1] of the two Acts of Congress which gave rise to the litigation in question, and that his argument, therefore, required him to show that the meaning which he attributed to the term, rather than one of the others, was its true meaning in the clause of the Constitution upon which he was commenting.

Perhaps it will not be thought unreasonable to place against the *dictum* in question the *dictum* of Webster in another case,[2] also decided by Chief Justice Marshall. It is true that he was arguing for a client; but then it was not his habit, even as counsel, to state propositions of law which he did not believe to be true, and the truth of which he was not prepared to maintain. He said:[3] "What is Florida? It is no part of the United States. How can it be? How is it represented? Do the laws of the United States reach Florida? Not unless by particular provisions. The Territory and all within it are to be governed by the acquiring power, except where there are reservations by the treaty. . . . Florida was to be governed by Congress as she thought proper. What has Congress done? She might have done anything, — she might have refused a trial by jury, and refused a legislature. . . . Does the law establishing the court at Key West come within the restrictions of the Constitution of the United States? If the Constitution does not extend over this territory, the law cannot be inconsistent with the national Constitution." It may be added that the decision was in Webster's favor, that not a word was said by the Chief Justice in disapproval of the passage just quoted, that Loughborough *v.* Blake was not cited either by counsel or judge, that it has seldom been cited by any member of the court by which it was decided, and that the *dictum* under consideration has, it is believed, never been so cited.

One other observation may be made upon Loughborough *v.* Blake, namely, that the District of Columbia differs materially from a Territory, that the former is within the limits of a State, was once a part of a State, and, therefore, the Constitution once

---

[1] Which enacts (sect. 1) "that a direct tax of $6,000,000 be and is hereby annually laid upon the United States, and the same shall be and is hereby apportioned to the States respectively in manner following: To the State of New Hampshire $193,586.74," etc. (enumerating the eighteen then existing States). Plainly, therefore, "United States" is here used in its original sense.

[2] Am. Ins. Co. *v.* Canter, 1 Pet. 511.   [3] 1 Pet. 538.

extended over it; and it may not be easy to show that it has ever ceased to extend over it.

The object of the 9th Section of Art. 1 is to prohibit Congress from doing certain things which it would otherwise have had the power to do under the several grants in the 8th section. Its object was, therefore, the same as that of the limitations contained in Section 8, and hence it would be as irrational to give Section 9 a more extensive operation, in respect to territory, than Section 8 has as it would be to give to the limitations upon the power of Congress imposed by Section 8 upon the grants contained in that section a more extensive operation than the grants themselves have.

An examination of the different subsections of Section 9 (other than subsection 1, which, having ceased to be operative, may be passed over) will lead to the same conclusion. Thus, subsection 2 provides that the writ of *Habeas Corpus* shall not be suspended, except under special circumstances; subsection 3, that no bill of attainder or *ex post facto* law shall be passed; subsection 4, that all "capitation or other direct" taxes which shall be laid shall be apportioned among the States according to the respective numbers of their inhabitants, *i. e.*, shall neither be laid upon property without reference to State lines, nor apportioned among the States according to their property;[1] subsection 5, that no tax or duty shall be laid on articles exported *from any State;* subsection 6, that no preference shall be given by any regulation of commerce or revenue to the ports of one State over those of another, and that no vessel bound to or from one State shall be obliged to enter, clear, or pay duties in another; subsection 7, that no money shall be drawn from the Treasury but in consequence of appropriations made by law, and a regular statement and account of the receipts and expenditures of all public money shall be published from time to time; and subsection 8, that no title of nobility shall be granted by the United States, and that no person holding any office of trust or profit under them shall accept of any present, emolument, office, or title from any King, Prince, or foreign State.

Of these seven subsections, no one discloses any intention to make it operative over a greater extent of territory than any of the others, and it must, therefore, be assumed that the intention was,

---

[1] By Article 8 of the Confederation, the amount of money required by Congress to be raised, from time to time, was to be apportioned among the States according to the aggregate value of the land in the States respectively, exclusive of crown lands.

in that respect, the same as to all; and hence it follows that they must all receive the same construction, in respect to the extent of territory over which they shall be operative, at least so far as their construction in that respect depends upon intention. Moreover, subsections 5 and 6 show conclusively upon their face that they are to be operative only within the States, and subsection 4 shows the same intention with sufficient clearness. Subsection 4 has also the same *raison d'être* as the limitations in subsections 1 and 4 of Section 8, *i. e.*, it was designed to secure a minority of wealthy States against the risk of having the whole burden of government thrown upon them by the less wealthy majority; and, therefore, it is absurd to suppose that it was intended to be operative in territories, — which were never to have any voice in Congress, and as to which, therefore, no such precaution was necessary.

Subsection 8 of Section 9 is more doubtful as to the territorial extent of its operation than any other part of the Constitution, — not because of any intention that can be justly attributed to its authors, but because of the language in which it happens to be couched. Thus, it provides in effect, that no title of nobility shall ever be granted by the United States as a sovereign, and that no person holding office under the sovereignty of the United States shall accept any present, etc. Fortunately, however, this subsection is of little importance, and any doubt that may exist as to its true construction, as it arises from accident, can have no influence upon the construction of other parts of the Constitution.

In respect to the first ten Amendments of the Constitution, it seems scarcely necessary to say more than to refer briefly to the circumstances under which they were adopted. They were proposed by the first Congress and at its first session, and were a concession to the party which had opposed the adoption of the Constitution, and which had thus far prevented its ratification by two of the States, namely, Rhode Island and North Carolina. Some of the States also which had ratified it, had done so only because they had been induced to believe that it would be amended at the earliest opportunity.

In respect to the nature and objects of the amendments adopted, it may be said that they are in the nature of a bill of rights, *i. e.*, they were designed still further to limit and restrict the powers of the new government under the grants contained in the first three articles of the Constitution, and especially those contained in the

8th section of Art. 1. It would be very surprising, therefore, if they should disclose any intention to extend their operation beyond the limits of the States; and in fact they do not disclose any such intention. If any doubt exists as to the extent of territory over which any of them are operative, it is only as to the 1st Amendment,[1] and it arises, not from any doubt as to the intention of its authors, but from the same cause as in subsection 8 of Section 9 of Art. 1. As to the remaining first ten Amendments, the utmost that can be said against the view now urged is that the language in which they are couched is so broad and general as to make them susceptible of an indefinite extension in respect to territory; but that is far from being sufficient to overcome the presumption which exists in favor of their being limited to the States. Moreover, it is as true of the first ten Amendments as it is of the 9th Section of Art. 1, that the intention of their authors was the same as to all of them, so far as regards the extent of territory over which they were to be operative; and yet it is certain that some of them are limited in their operation to the States. Thus, the 6th Amendment provides that all criminal trials shall be by a jury of the "State and district" in which the crime shall have been committed;[2] and by "district" is here meant either an entire State or a subdivision of a State. So the 7th Amendment perpetuates the right to trial by jury in common-law actions, and declares that no fact tried by a jury shall be otherwise re-examined in any court of the United States than according to the rules of the common law. It is assumed, therefore, that the common law of England will be the law of the land in every place where this amendment will be operative. Moreover, the operation of the amendment is expressly limited to courts of the United States, *i. e.*, courts exercising some portion of the judicial power conferred upon the United States by Art. 3 of the Constitution; and it is only within the States, as has been seen,[3] that such power can be exercised, or such courts can exist. Lastly, the 10th Amendment provides that the powers not delegated to the United States by the Constitution (*i. e.*, in its first three articles), nor prohibited by it to the States (*i. e.*, in Section 10

---

[1] "Congress shall make no law respecting an establishment of religion, or prohibiting the free exercise thereof; or abridging the freedom of speech, or of the press; or the right of the people peaceably to assemble, and to petition the government for a redress of grievances."

[2] U. S. *v.* Dawson, 15 How. 467.   [3] See *supra*, page 378.

of Art. 1), are reserved to the States respectively or to the people (*i. e.*, the people of the respective States); and there could not well be a stronger proof that the sole object of the first ten amendments was to limit the power of the United States in and over the several States. Nor should the fact be lost sight of that these ten amendments as a whole are so peculiarly and so exclusively English that an immediate and compulsory application of them to ancient and thickly settled Spanish colonies would furnish as striking a proof of our unfitness to govern dependencies, or to deal with alien races, as our bitterest enemies could desire.

It may be added that Art. 3, Section 2, subsection 3, is of the same nature as the first ten Amendments; and yet that subsection is limited, like the 7th Amendment, to the courts of the United States, and so to the several States, and that, too, not only for reasons applicable to the whole of Art. 3, but because it is expressly provided that all trials for crimes shall be held in the State where the crime was committed; and though it is added that, when not committed in any State, the trial shall be at such place as Congress by law directs, yet a crime not committed in a State can come within that subsection only when it is committed on the high seas, or in some place which is without an organized government, and so without the means of administering justice.[1]

It must be admitted that the provisions, both of the original Constitution and of the amendments, securing the right of trial by jury, have several times been subjects of discussion in the Supreme Court, and that opinions have been expressed by members of that court that these provisions extend to Territories. But, in the recent case of the American Publishing Co. *v.* Fisher,[2] the question was treated as still an open one; and though, in the still more recent case of Thompson *v.* Utah,[3] the court professedly decided that the provisions in question extended to the former territory of Utah, yet it seems clear that the question was not involved in the decision. The only question directly involved was whether the clause in the constitution of Utah, providing that persons accused of felonies not capital should be tried by a jury of eight persons, was *ex post facto* as to a felony committed while

---

[1] See U. S. *v.* Jones, 137 U. S. 202; Cook *v.* U. S., 138 U. S. 157, 181. It seems clear also that the Constitution intended that Congress, in directing the place of trial of a crime not committed in any State, should select a place within the limits of some State, as otherwise the trial could not be in a United States court.

[2] 166 U. S. 464.   [3] 170 U. S. 343.

Utah was a territory, and, therefore, inoperative; and that question was decided in the affirmative, and for the reason that the law of the Territory, as it was when the crime was committed, required any person accused of such a crime to be tried by a jury of twelve persons. But, if such was the law of the Territory, it seems to have been immaterial how it was established, — whether by the Constitution of the United States, or by Act of Congress, or by Act of the territorial legislature; and, in fact, such was the law of the Territory by virtue of an Act of the territorial legislature,[1] and therefore it was not necessary for the accused to invoke the aid of the Constitution of the United States.[2]

It may aid us in determining the status of our new territories to inquire what their status would be, if the United States, instead of being a confederation of States, were a single State, organized substantially as our several States are, or if it were a monarchy, either absolute or constitutional.

The mere acquisition by one country (A, for example) of the sovereignty over another country (B, for example) produces no other legal effect upon the latter than to give it a new sovereign, and consequently to substitute the legislature and the chief executive of A for those of B; but A and B will still be in strictness foreign to each other, each having its own government, laws, and institutions; and though the legislature and chief executive of each will be the same, yet they will act in an entirely different capacity when acting for B from that in which they act when acting for A.[3] If any greater change than this is wrought, it will be because A has done something more to B than to acquire the sovereignty over her. She may do with B whatever she pleases, assuming the sovereignty which she has acquired over her to be absolute. She may (for example) incorporate B so completely with A that B's own government, institutions, and laws will cease to

---

[1] See 170 U. S. 345. Moreover, by the Act of Sept. 9, 1850, c. 51, s. 17 (9 Stats. 435, 458), for organizing the Territory of Utah, it was enacted as follows: "The Constitution and laws of the United States are hereby extended over and declared to be in force in said Territory of Utah, so far as the same, or any provision thereof, may be applicable." And though it was not within the power of Congress to extend the Constitution over territory to which it did not extend by its own force, yet Congress could give it the effect of a statute in such territory, and that was the effect of this provision.

[2] In Am. Ins. Co. v. Canter, 1 Pet. 511, 538, Webster, *arguendo*, said Congress had the power to refuse trial by jury to the Territory of Florida. See *supra*, page 382.

[3] Hence, no statute made by the legislature of A as such will affect B, unless it expressly declare that it shall extend to B. See *supra*, page 382.

exist, and even she herself will cease to exist as a separate country; or A may keep the two countries entirely separate and distinct, and yet reduce the inhabitants of B to a condition of servitude. But if B be incorporated with A, or the inhabitants of B be reduced to a condition of servitude, it will not be because of the acquisition by A of the sovereignty over B, but because of the action taken by A consequent upon the acquisition of such sovereignty. If, indeed, A have a written constitution, by which her government was created and organized, and under which it acts, and the powers of such government are subject to limitations imposed by the constitution, and such limitations are made by the constitution to apply to all future acquisitions of territory, and so are applicable to B, of course it will follow that the government of A will be subject to the same limitations when acting for B as when acting for A; and A can get rid of these limitations, in respect either to herself or B, only by changing or overthrowing her constitution.

Does, then, the fact that the United States is a confederation of States make any difference? It is conceived that it makes no difference whatever as to the foregoing principles; but it does suggest two observations which affect their application: first, that, as all the limitations imposed upon the United States by the Constitution have reference primarily to the States, and owe their existence primarily to the fact that the sovereignty over the territory of each State is divided between the State and the United States, there is a strong presumption that such limitations have no application to territory which is subject to no State sovereignty, and in which the United States can exercise all the power which can be exercised within a State either by the State or by the United States; secondly, that there is but one known mode of incorporating newly acquired territory into the United States, namely, by admitting it as a State.

Much confusion of ideas has been caused as to the effect of the acquisition of new territory by the United States, by the constant use of the word "annexation," — a word which has no constitutional or legal meaning. It first came into general use in connection with the agitation for and against the acquisition of Texas. Whether its use was by design or accident may not be certain. The acquisition of Texas was peculiar in this, namely, that it was the first instance (as it is still the only instance) of the acquisition of foreign territory by admitting it as a State. For this reason, the word "admission" may have been thought objectionable, that word having become associated with the practice of admitting as States territory already within the sovereignty of the United States. The acquisition of Texas was peculiar also in another respect, namely, that it was the acquisition of an independent State with her own consent. In this respect, the case of Hawaii is similar to that of Texas; and this may account for the fact that Hawaii was acquired by the process (so called) of annexation.[1] But, however this may be, the mode in which Hawaii was acquired does not at all affect her *status* when acquired, nor make it different from that of the Spanish islands which have been acquired by conquest and by treaty with Spain.

What has been the practice of Congress in respect to those branches of legislation which the Constitution[2] requires to be uniform throughout the United States, and does such practice indicate that Congress has held itself bound by the Constitution to make such legislation uniform throughout all territory within the sovereignty of the United States? First, the undoubted fact that there has been hitherto no want of uniformity in the taxes, duties, imposts, and excises laid and collected by Congress, nor in the rules of naturalization, or the laws on the subject of bankruptcies, established by Congress, proves nothing; for there has not hitherto been the slightest reason why legislation upon each of these subjects should not be uniform throughout all the territory over which it extended; nor have there been even two opinions upon the question. Secondly, the earliest legislation respecting duties upon imports and tonnage[3] was limited in its operation to the States. This, however, may not have involved any constitutional question, as it did not follow that there was to be "free trade" between the territories and foreign countries, but rather that foreign goods could not enter the territories at all, for want of any ports of entry.[4]

---

[1] Another point of similarity between Texas and Hawaii is, that both were acquired by joint resolution. The resolution of March 1, 1845, by which Texas was acquired (5 Stats. 797) is entitled, "Joint Resolution for annexing Texas to the United States;" but neither the verb "annex," nor the noun "annexation," occurs in the resolution itself. The resolution of July 7, 1898, by which Hawaii was acquired, is entitled, "Joint Resolution to provide for annexing the Hawaiian Islands to the United States;" and the resolution itself declares "that the said Hawaiian Islands and their dependencies be, and they are hereby annexed as a part of the territory of the United States, and are subject to the sovereign dominion thereof."

[2] Art. 1, sec. 8, subsects. 1 and 4.

[3] Acts of July 31, 1789, ch. 5 (1 Stats. 29), and Aug. 4, 1790, ch. 57 (1 Stats. 145).

[4] There was, however, early legislation imposing excise duties, and this was also

The earliest legislation respecting naturalization [1] and bankruptcy [2] was also limited in its operation to the States; and it seems that this was in violation of the Constitution, if "United States," as used in Art. 1, Section 8, subsection 4, includes the territories; for a consequence was that no person residing in a territory could be naturalized, and that neither any debtor residing in a territory, nor the creditors of any such debtor, could have the benefit of the bankrupt law. Thirdly, all naturalization acts except the first, and all bankrupt acts except the first, have been extended to the territories, but it by no means follows that Congress regarded itself as bound by the Constitution so to extend them. So also the Act of March 2, 1799,[3] to regulate the collection of duties on imports and tonnage, was extended to the then existing territories, *i. e.*, the latter were divided into collection districts; and this is true also of all similar acts which have since been passed, and of all territories which have since been acquired; and, if Congress had not taken this course, it must have either prohibited the importation of foreign goods into territories, or it must have admitted all foreign goods free of duty, or it must have established for the territories a revenue system of their own. Moreover, there were many reasons in favor of the course adopted, and none in favor of either of the other three: First, all the different parcels of territory acquired by the United States from time to time (with the unimportant exception of Alaska) were contiguous either to existing States or to territory previously acquired; secondly, none of them differed more widely from the States in soil and climate than the States differed from each other; thirdly, they were all virtually without inhabitants and were expected to be peopled by immigrants from the States, from the British Islands, and from Western Europe; fourthly, they were all expected, at an early day, to be formed into States, and as such to be admitted into the Union; fifthly, none of them produced (to any extent) dutiable articles which, if admitted into the United States free of duty, would either deprive the government of revenue, or compete with home products, or produce both of these effects; sixthly, they all bordered upon navi-

---

limited to the States. See Act of March 3, 1791, ch. 81 (1 Stats. 199). It seems, therefore, that such legislation was in violation of Art. 1 of the Constitution, Sec. 8, subsect. 1, if "United States," as used in that subsection, includes territories, as no excise duties were imposed upon the latter.

[1] Act of March 26, 1790, ch. 29, 1 Stats. 103.
[2] Act of April 4, 1800, ch. 19, 2 Stats. 19.   [3] 1 Stats. 627.

gable waters through which the products of all foreign countries could easily be imported into them, and, if admitted free of duty, could be smuggled thence into the States.[1]

With the acquisition of Hawaii and the Spanish islands, however, all these conditions are radically changed. None of these islands have been acquired with a view to their being admitted as States, and it is to be sincerely hoped that they never will be so admitted, *i. e.*, that they will never be permitted to share in the government of this country, and especially to be represented in the United States Senate. Their agricultural capabilities are very great, their products enter almost wholly into commerce, and all or nearly all of them are dutiable under our tariff. Some of them consist of articles from which the government raises a great amount of revenue, and most of them, if admitted free of duty, will compete ruinously with home products of the same kind. Lastly, none of these islands are manufacturing countries, nor are likely to become such, and none of them import articles which compete with their home products, and, therefore, duties should be levied on articles imported into them only for purposes of revenue.

The strongest possible reasons, therefore, exist for abandoning totally, in respect to our new territories, the practice which has hitherto prevailed of extending to territories the revenue system of the United States, and for giving to each of them a revenue system of its own.[2] This is required as well in justice to them as in justice to this country; for, while the admission of sugar and tobacco, for example, from those islands into this country free of duty, would ruin the producers of those articles in this country, and would make it necessary for the government to resort to new and oppressive modes of raising revenue, the extension to those islands of our tariff on imports would compel their people to buy

---

[1] On the 14th of August, 1848, the then military governor of California wrote to the War Department as follows: "If all customs were withdrawn, and the ports thrown open free to the world, San Francisco would be made the depot of all the foreign goods in the North Pacific, to the injury of our revenue and the interests of our own merchants." See Cross *v.* Harrison, 16 How. 164, 183.

[2] Congress seems to have taken it for granted that the revenue system of the United States was to be extended to the Hawaiian Islands; for the resolution by which those islands were acquired declares that "until legislation shall be enacted extending the United States customs laws and regulations to the Hawaiian Islands, the existing customs relations of the Hawaiian Islands with the United States and other countries shall remain unchanged."

imported articles, not as their interests, but as our interests, dictate.

If we are to undertake the government of dependent countries, with any hope of gaining credit for ourselves, we must enter upon the task with a single eye to promoting the interests of the people governed, and we must content ourselves with such material advantages as may accrue to us incidentally from a faithful discharge of our duty. Does the Constitution of the United States prevent our attempting such a rôle? If it does, one will be driven to the conclusion that the authors of that instrument were either less successful in saying what they meant, or else were less sagacious and far-sighted, than they have had the reputation of being.

C. C. Langdell.

NOTE.

THE numerous editions of the Constitution of the United States vary somewhat in their mode of dividing the different sections into paragraphs, and in numbering the paragraphs. For example, in Art. 1, Section 9, some editions print in one paragraph the matter which, in the preceding article, is treated as constituting subsections 5 and 6; and this, of course, changes the numbering of the remaining paragraphs. So in Art. 2, Section 1, some editions do not number the third paragraph, it having been superseded by the 12th Amendment. Some editions also print and number the form of oath at the end of the section as a separate paragraph. In the preceding article the third paragraph is regarded as numbered, and the form of oath is not regarded as a separate paragraph; and hence the section is referred to as containing eight subsections.

www.ingramcontent.com/pod-product-compliance
Lightning Source LLC
Chambersburg PA
CBHW021957170526
45157CB00003B/1034